The Henry Williamson Soc

Number 34 September 1998

Reality in War Literature

The Henry Williamson Society Journal
Issue 34 September 1998
© Published by HWS ISSN C144-9338
ISBN 1 873507 13 5

COPY DATES
For Spring Newsletter: 7 January 1999
For Autumn Journal: 1 April 1999

Please send a short biographical note with all items

Material to be submitted for publication should be typed (double-spaced), bearing the writer's name and address.
Where possible please send a diskette with your hard (i.e. typed) copy and state the software used. We have moved into the modern age.
Length of articles by negotiation. Contributions are not normally returned.
Articles, correspondence and review copies of books should be sent to the Editor.

CONTENTS

Cover Illustration by C.R.W. Nevinson.
We are grateful to Mrs Anne Patterson, the Copyright Holder, for permission to reproduce this work owned by the Henry Williamson Literary Estate.

Hut illustration on Title Page by Peter Rothwell
Back cover replica of poster designed for the Society by Anne Williamson

EDITORIAL

This issue of the *Journal* commemorates the eightieth anniversary of the ending of the First World War. Containing a selection of material too detailed to be accommodated in my new book *A Patriot's Progress: Henry Williamson and the First World War*[1] it is thus virtually a supplement to it. Henry Williamson's writings on the First World War[2] constitute a vivid portrait of that era – and are superb examples of reality in war literature.

You will see that the facsimile copy of the manuscript of Henry Williamson's essay 'Reality in War Literature' is signed and dated 12.12.26. This early date might surprise those of you who are accustomed to the version in *The Linhay on the Downs*. Henry tried without success to place this essay in several journals including *The Ypres Times*, whose editor wrote to say that he felt it would 'fit uneasily' between their covers. But the publication of *Tarka* in 1927, the subsequent award of the Hawthornden Prize and the ensuing tenth anniversary of the ending of the First World War, meant Henry was able to take advantage of the publicity to publish several articles with the war as their subject. 'Reality in War Literature' was taken by *The London Mercury* and published in January 1929. The final version which was printed in *The Linhay on the Downs*[3] is much expanded from the original essay and is the one under consideration in the following discussion.

'Reality in War Literature' is interesting in its own right as an example of critical writing and in showing us Henry's thoughts about the books in this genre by his contemporaries. But this major essay is even more interesting for what one can infer from its content. As I have remarked in the closing paragraphs of *A Patriot's Progress*, Williamson sets out in this essay his criteria for the book that would stand up against Tolstoi's *War and Peace*. He suggests *Le Feu* by Henri Barbusse as the nearest approximation and proceeds to compare his selection of books against *Le Feu* to their detriment. I have already examined the deep influence of Henri Barbusse and *Le Feu* in *A Patriot's Progress* and don't wish to labour that point here but rather to give emphasis to the over-ruling standard Henry makes of Tolstoi's *War and Peace*. Williamson is stating in this essay that there had not been at that point a book to equal *War and Peace* encapsulating 'the sense of reality in action, verging on the unreal ...' and the inference is, albeit obliquely and with great skill, that it would be his own work on 'war and peace' that would stand against that test. Henry, of course, already knew what he was planning to write – his readers still had many years to wait to be able to understand his inference.

Williamson came back to this theme in a more obvious manner in the 'War and Peace' chapter of *Lucifer Before Sunrise*[4], where over Christmas 1941 Phillip reads the book bought many years before but never read until that moment 'what had generally been claimed to be the greatest novel in the world – Tolstoi's *War and Peace*'. (I am quite sure Henry himself read the book at the time of his original essay and that he actually re-read it in 1941.) Reading it sharpens Phillip's thoughts about his own series of novels waiting to be written and he realises that 'the comprehensive novel had not been written because he had not developed the comprehensive vision to see the war of 1914-18 and the decades preceding it as a human entity.' As the year changes from 1941 to 1942, Phillip sits before the fire in the parlour of the Norfolk Farm, ruminating over the rights and wrongs of the Second World War and he thinks of the

> *writer of genius who would recreate the miseries and hopes of the times as did Tolstoi in another age, in his great novel. That Russian nobleman shut himself away for over five years and with infinite care and patience, while sustaining within himself the power to endure, set his mind to bring alive within the pages of his story the peasants and the landowners, the ministers and the priests, the battles and the sufferings, the lovers and deaths and joys and tragedies of an entire Russian generation: more, of an entire European age. There was Napoleon with his new order for Europe, directing battles and regarding the dead and the wounded – all in* War and Peace *... . If I do not survive this war, who will write a novel of our times, transcending* War and Peace*? ... He must deal truly, otherwise with comprehension and clarity, with the inner and psychological processes ... . He must create character, environment and action out of a common humanity and relate all the effects of peace to all the causes of war... .*

This is Henry Williamson's *cri de coeur* for the recognition that it is *A Chronicle of Ancient Sunlight*, which encompasses both the First and Second World Wars, that it is *his* great novel series that is the answer to his own rhetorical question in 'Reality in War Literature' – who will write a book that is equal to Tolstoi's *War and Peace*?

C.P. Snow wrote an illuminating essay on Tolstoy (the more usual English spelling) in his book *The Realists*[5] in which we find a statement that gives a direct analogy between these two writers. Snow examines Tolstoy's method for writing:

> *It is set down with the* truth *which was his first demand for his own art or ... anyone else's. He didn't believe in invention. In his personal and intense vision, he didn't believe in imagination. That is, imagination ordinarily conceived. What was* there *was more marvellous than anything one's feeble mind could construct; though one's mind could be given a chance to interpret or analyse the novel. That was his artistic freedom. It gave him the certainty of his God's eye surveillance.* [cf. Henry's 'to see as the sun sees, without shadows']
>
> *Thus we know about his childhood .... For the military history and the social data of a period the generation before his own, he used, like any sane writer setting out upon an epic, every source he could absorb. His chief source was his own family. There, true to his credo, he invented very little ... he changed the name of his mother. She was actually the Princess Marya Volkonsky. With a daring stroke of invention, her son transmuted this name into Bolkonsky .... With comparable ingenuity, Dorokhov ... was transmuted into Dolokhov. ... Tolstoy's father Nikolai appears in the novel as Nikolai Rostov, as faithfully as Tolstoy could manage, which is as faithfully as any writer could manage.'*

So here is direct analogy, not just in the intent and compass of the two works but in almost identical method. Count Leo Tolstoy lived from 1828 to 1910. *War and Peace* was written between 1863-9, soon after his marriage to Sonya Behr, who took over the running of his large estate to free him to concentrate on his epic work. Tolstoy's preparations for the book were prodigious, as were Williamson's to be a century later.

In the Preface to his book, Snow sets out his analysis of Realism: 'In the great realistic novels, there is a presiding, unconcealed, interpreting intelligence. They are all of them concerned with the actual social setting in which their personages exist. The concrete world, the world of physical fact, the shapes of society are essential to the art. The people have to be projected ... but also examined with the writer's psychological resources and with cognitive intelligence. Both those components are features of realism.' To me, this is exactly the same thought that Henry Williamson expresses in 'Reality in War Literature' and even more directly in the 'War and Peace' chapter of *Lucifer Before Sunrise.*

With the publication of *A Patriot's Progress: Henry Williamson and the First World War* a direct comparison can be made at last between Henry's own experience and that of Phillip Maddison in the war volumes of the *Chronicle.* Now we can see that Henry's purpose went far beyond recording his own small part in that war – that his intent in *A Chronicle of Ancient Sunlight* was to show the total reality of war, its causes and effects, in war and in peace. But beyond that even, the reality of Henry Williamson's writings on the First World War are a testament to all those who took part in that war as lasting as the stone monuments engraved with names in every village and town and war cemetery.

AW

NOTES

1. Anne Williamson, *A Patriot's Progress: Henry Williamson and the First World War*, Sutton Publishing, September 1998, £18.99. ISBN 0 7509 1339 8.
2. *The Wet Flanders Plain, The Patriot's Progress*, the five 'war' volumes of *A Chronicle of Ancient Sunlight*, and not forgetting his numerous articles on the subject.
3. Henry Williamson, *The Linhay on the Downs and Other Stories*, Cape 1934. 'Reality in War Literature', pp 224-62. Photocopies of this article can be obtained from the HWS Publications Manager (address on inside back cover),
   price £1.50.
4. Henry Williamson, *Lucifer Before Sunrise*, (Vol. 14, *A Chronicle of Ancient Sunlight*, Macdonald, 1967, chapter 14, 'War and Peace', pp 22-223.
5. C.P. Snow, *The Realists: Portraits of Eight Novelists*, Macmillan, 1978. 'Tolstoy', pp 139-66.

As you will see, there is no room for explanatory notes for the items included in this issue, so I hope they are all obvious. Some are cross-referenced from my new book (as above Note 1); others are facsimile illustrations for which there was no room in the new book due to space restrictions.

Reality in War Literature

Henry Williamson

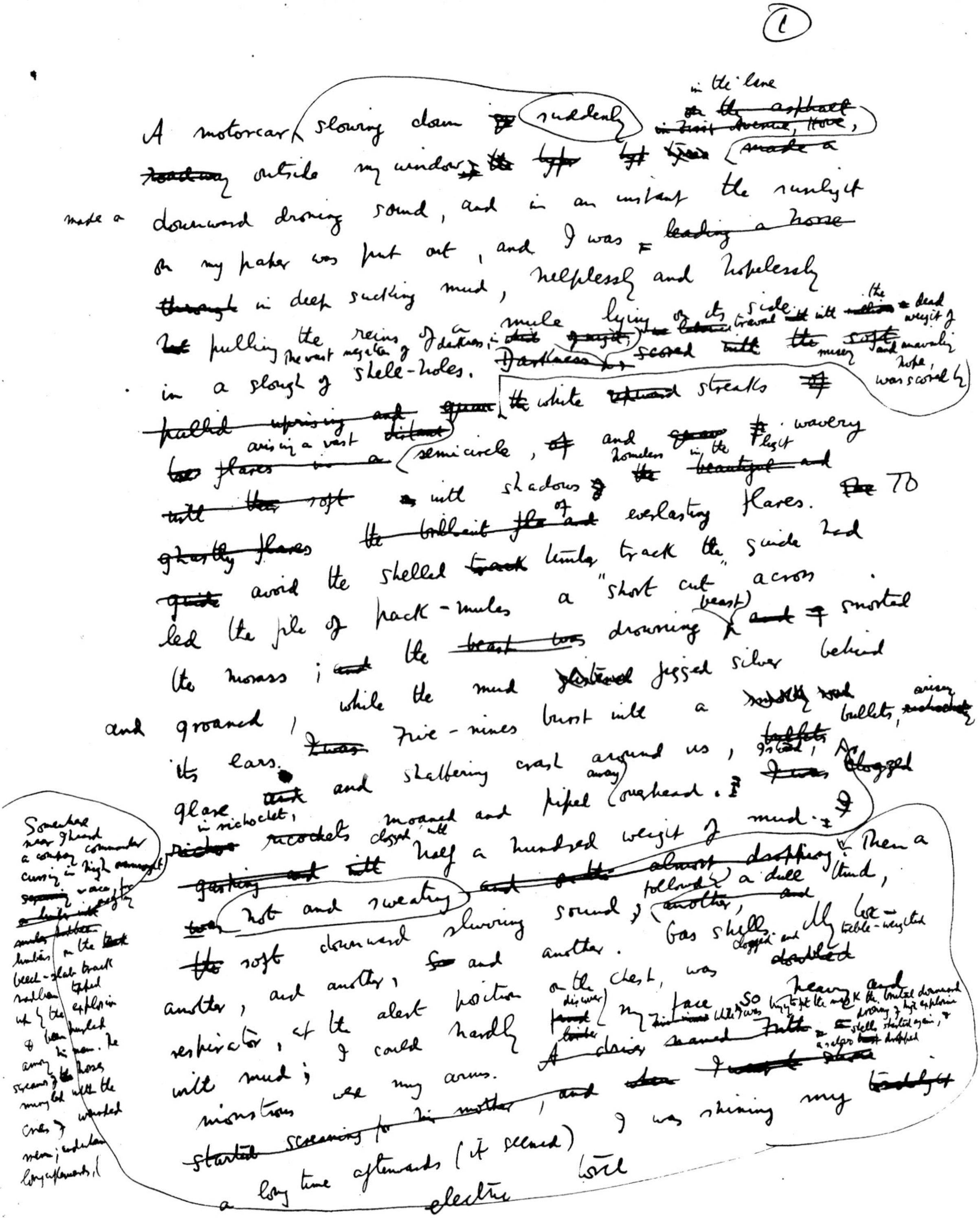

1

A motorcar slowing down suddenly in the lane, Hove, outside my window made a downward droning sound, and in an instant the sunlight on my paper was put out, and I was in deep sucking mud, helplessly and hopelessly pulling the reins of a mule lying on its side travail with the dead weight of the vast neglect of darkness; scored the misery and anxiety hope, was scored by in a slough of shell-holes. the white streaks arising a vast semicircle, and homeless in the wavery light with shadows of everlasting flares. TO avoid the shelled limber track the guide had led the file of pack-mules a "short cut" across the morass; the beast drowning snorted and groaned, while the mud jagged silver behind its ears. Five-nines burst with a and shattering crash around us, bullets, awry glare and piped away overhead. in richochet, moaned and ricochets clogged with half a hundred weight of mud. Then a hot and sweating followed a dull thud, the soft downward slurring sound, another, and another. Gas shells. My box-respirator, at the alert position on the chest, was so heavy with mud; I could hardly discover my face see my arms. I was shining my monstrous screaming a long time afterwards (it seemed) electric torch

Somewhere near I heard a company commander cursing in high voice ... on the limber (beech-slab track) ... explosion ... the screaming of the horse ... wounded men; ambulance ...

tangled and twisted with shreds of his waterproof cape, ②
(head and) ~~working in~~ ~~and~~ in a trough of dark red slime.

on his legs, ~~twisted~~ and [illegible] ~~under the~~ ~~amongst the~~ ~~red gallon of red paint~~ ~~chucked over~~ ~~cape~~ ~~the~~ ~~a~~ ~~waterproof~~ ~~semblance of what might have been a wet red jacket.~~ ~~Then~~ ~~a torn waterproof cape. Then a~~ ~~struggling~~ ~~horse~~ ~~staggered~~ ~~with unnatural appendages~~ mule ~~I~~ ~~wounded~~ (~~screaming~~ ~~horse~~ and ~~most~~ under it and broke, and staggered,) ~~[illegible]~~ ~~trodden~~ Drive forth sank ~~into~~ into reared up ~~and most~~

the slough.

Nothing ~~much~~ at all, ~~as the Salie~~ as life in the Salient went; an ~~the~~ any ordinary incident in ~~a first line~~ the night job of ~~[illegible]~~ infantry ~~for~~ ~~first line~~ transport. Afterwards those 8-hour journeys ~~seen~~ seemed ~~almost~~ cushy, compared with ~~life~~ the ~~outposts~~ front line of outposts during Third Ypres.

The noise of ~~the~~ a motorcar, suddenly slowing down ~~in~~ ~~the~~ ~~suddenly~~ in our First Avenue roadway in this year of peace nineteen twenty six put out the sunlight for a millionth part of second; I admit ~~As~~ the that I encourage the visitation of old scenes of the war. ~~The~~ ~~indescribable~~ ~~glance~~ sunlight, ~~being~~ an agent of life, is often stronger than the haunting will to be back again; ~~night and [illegible]~~ predict darkness in the last time. Yet I have sat for hours in the ~~after~~ afternoon summer sunshine on Rockham beach ~~in~~ near Morte Hoe in North Devon, ~~sent~~ (from a boy's catapult) at a round shooting small irregular pebbles, hearing them rise ~~bowed~~ bowedar, for the psychic pleasure of fall with the chromatic whizzing and ~~moaning~~ piping, and when it was time to ~~whining~~ whining of spent bullets. And when it was ~~[illegible]~~ spheres at swim and throw seaweed at my friends against at ~~an~~ ~~apex of the~~ an ~~apex~~ upward ~~back~~ ~~into~~ ~~deeds~~ the wave-line, ~~I threw~~ flicked pebbles in their ~~way~~ too thralled in deep from me, and I knew that ~~me~~ too
crying flight, and I knew
~~awaited~~ dreadful night.

(3)

~~At~~ (One smell of) ~~wood~~ Smoke from a wood fire, and I am back again in the German dugouts ~~alas~~ above the Ancre Valley, with smarting eyes; ~~the downs of the~~ ~~Sussex ... have a chalky subsoil, and~~ memories and visions that return at the smell of a fire of bits of ~~pine wood~~ ~~dead~~ ~~wood~~ dead planks or boxes would fill a hundred pages; ~~of the Times;~~ ~~the battle written;~~ ~~but they~~ [until] be written, and then perhaps ~~places~~ ~~one day;~~ ~~perhaps~~ one day they haunt no more. Unless by ~~then will~~ then another ~~generation of~~ phantom generation has arisen and goes to their ~~forefathers~~ fathers. ~~that I can~~

Sometimes, but very occasionally, I find ~~a~~ ~~book is written that~~ a book that I can shut myself away with, ~~book~~ locking the door of my writing room, earthing the switch of the wireless set, cursing (~~that~~ old Salient habit) when my gentle wife comes to say it is ~~tea~~ time for tea, or supper, or bed, and that it will be so tired again ... two or three in the morning again, a dead fire, no use, everything empty and grey.

Way of Revelation got me that way; and perhaps it was as well that ~~it~~ Capt. Ewart's ~~publishers~~ publishers did not print it in its original length, which was three times that of the published volume. Or it might have been better, for the rejected two-thirds was so uneven, that one would have had to pause. The publishers compared it to Tolstoy's War and Peace, but it ~~was~~ ~~comparison~~ no comparison, as was proved by its reception by the critics, who did not need to ~~take~~ ~~their~~ groan for an attitude when reviewing it, but

wrote, naturally out of their excitations. And these
emotions, being reflected back again upon poor Ewart, who in his
war-wracked state could
~~the~~ (of just support
his own, ~~helped to~~ ~~aided~~ ~~were~~ brought on his collapse. Yes,
darkness gets back again if it can, by many ways.

How many people, who care for the real stuff (as
opposed to ~~the~~ emotionalism of people who went three overbrimming
into verse and prose about heroes, sacred emblems, the scales
of justice, etc etc) have read Mr Patrick Miller's The Natural
Man? It may be out of print now; but I suggest that it is time
it was reprinted. After disappointing and artificial displays like
the films Mons and Ypres, to which ~~...~~ ~~...~~ people
flocked in millions, it is surely indicated that the time
has come when war books will be brought and read and
kept. The book of the War has yet to be written — I mean the
story of the ordinary man written with plain seeing (the rarest thing in
the world) it would be the story of nearly every
~~fighting~~ militarised man in Europe. Everyone was somebody's son.

To return to the Natural Man. It is true, to my mind, the ~~the~~ ~~detailed~~ ~~description~~
~~...~~ It has one blemish, Paris leave is too
well written. The incident of the prostitute during Paris leave and incidents, the
detailed and prolonged. The war scenes and incidents, and other
characters of the 18-pdr. battery, Crump, Saxon, Blaven, Chard, are so interesting that the hint.
opinions of the interruption. So, it may be answered, did (apparently always!)
one resent the interruption so engaged; I wish Mr Miller
Blaven, the natural man do sturdy book; revise the next edition and add
the War. A fine world ~~...~~ further scenes that would fill
in some of the

(5

disappointing gaps where he breaks off a carefully built
up scene during its most interesting moments. It's bad
technique to do this. The reader shouts "Go on, don't stop"; ~~and~~
but vainly.

Let me quote, from _The Natural Man_, the (first) description of
the Salient, ~~before the~~ in the summer of 1917, before the
battles of that year.

Page 118 – 119, 120.

—

Innumerable many people have read the three war books
by Mr R. H. Mottram – _The Spanish Farm_, _Sixty Four Ninety Four!_,
and _The Crime of at Vanderlynden's_. The first is the best;
the pendant books seem to me to have been written too
easily – a Sunday afternoon, after roast beef and Yorkshire
pudding – that typical (lazy) middle-class Sunday afternoon that
Mr Mottram has so well indicated in his (last) recently
printed short story of d'Archville. The books are interesting,
but they sag with comfort; the battle scenes, are ~~feeble~~
lazily feeble. Perhaps they are imaginary. They won't do.

Mr H. M. Tomlinson has said that Mr
Mottram's book, or books, are the finest that have come out
of the War. His war library must be small.

Mr Tomlinson, I believe, was a War correspondent

(6

during the War — that is, one ~~obey for those~~ of a
group whose first consideration was to unite in a
certain way. We were at war; the people must be
heartened, etc. The ordinary war correspondent conceded
unite; he could not "see plain"; he wrote often in an
emotional state, and ~~his~~ the result usually coincided
with what millions of unhappy people at home
thought the the ultimate truth of the universe. Every
~~country~~ nation in the war thought that, in varying degrees;
and sometimes I am filled with a black and bitter dread
that those old ways of thinking (or assimilating ~~from~~ from
newspapers) will inevitably bring on another War...
~~but the ghosts are~~ Mr Tomlinson was not the ordinary
war correspondent. He has the gift of natural seeing. Let
me quote from his book _Waiting for Daylight_, from the
long essay called _The Nobodies_. It has the spirit that
is rare, and will come as a revelation to many
people who do not know Mr Tomlinson's work.

Page 118 — 121.

[I come now to three books of Mr Ford Madox
Ford — Mr Hueffer, he used to call himself. The
books are well known, Island unique. Mr Ford has
been writing a long time, and he is set in ~~his~~ those
peculiarities which seem to irritate some people. He
talks, as it were, with profound
reason and clarity;

(7.

moving and)
the middle of a beautifully presented
and suddenly [has a tendency] to howl and shout, and use Old Testament
scene, he language. Not
it and tell us another story about a that
called Sylvia Tietjens. It is good, but it
is original
are one of
the irritated but some of the
ejaculations seem superfluous. Quite life-like; but they are
a little [illegible] jar the reader's mood. I imagine that Mr Ford was reprimanded as a child.

The books are fragments of a long novel. They are called,
in order of seniority, Some do Not ("Some rest on Snowy Bosoms, Some
do not"), No more Parades, and A Man Could Stand
Up. The first must be read, for itself, and
for the better comprehension of No more Parades,
which is a magnificent description of an Infantry
Base Depot in France before the
Mad break-through in 1918. I imagine the story of
Captain Tietjens and his wife Sylvia
was intended as counterpoint to the war scenes; one
sustains the other in my memory. Yet I read
No more Parades for its descriptions, its clear and
vivid recreation of old scenes. I know
that base-camp. Mr Ford does not mar my memory
of it. He can write. I can't make out
the third book. It is made up of
three great instantaneous fragments. The middle
fragment is what confuses me. It is a
re-creation of a trench,
presumably somewhere south of
Kemmel Hill,

(8

in April 1918. The German drive ~~has taken~~ is over; ~~and~~ another (spirit) imbue of the) is imminent, and is expected ~~the next is expected to~~ to take Bailleul. ~~Secondly second~~ Minute by minute the trench scene is built up. ~~That at~~ It has a tremendous power of presentation to the reader. And what a scene! Pinkish gravel trenches, (Perhaps there were some, but ~~Tho~~ I see land of ~~them~~ or was it, gravel trenches in that ~~[illegible]~~ at sunrise, and the ~~remnant~~ battalion fixing bayonets in them, ~~crept to~~ ~~one long~~ line ~~in~~ (county) ~~a~~ in spite of the traverses & perhaps ~~a~~ sheering detailed a few ways further on. ~~stepping at smartly~~ ~~sight and more~~ et seq)

(Page 107

I have an uneasy feeling) ~~and deep gallows~~ about a writer of elderly talent when he Mr Ford, ~~who was in the Buffs during the war,~~ ~~he~~ who served during the war as a subaltern in the Buffs, ~~has~~ ~~[illegible]~~ ~~took~~ wrote ~~is~~ perpetrates a colossal fable when he not based ~~on~~ this trench fragment. That is to say, it is a (but why should it be?) called an actuality of experience. It has got the spirit of ~~a~~ reality, the muddle, inner voice. It is, in Conrad's phrase, the incoherence of actuality; ~~but~~ gradually, having "true but imaginary". Yes, but as I am a ~~an~~ remote & fleeting thought — that as an authority, arising ~~of~~ the book. It is fine, the characters cannot me as I read ~~it~~. ~~[illegible]~~ the incidents are fresh and are original, remain in the memory — even the

(9

~~deliberately~~ ~~written~~ ~~profound~~ [~~attentive~~] description of sandwiches
prepared for ~~acting~~ ~~Col~~ Captain (acting Major) Tietjens
in the trenches. Rather ~~a~~ ~~d~~ [meal is of] ~~in the~~ ~~classical manner~~ bears out the
described in the classical manner, and
of well-known part that man is an imitative creature.
'What a meal! How magnificently done!' ~~a~~ ~~potence~~ the
voice of posterity might well exclaim. Yes, the Ford [majesty] ~~intended~~
deliberately intended it the ~~[illegible]~~ done in the ~~purple manner~~ manner of ~~[illegible]~~ classic meals. ~~[illegible]~~.
~~did it~~ ~~magnificently~~.

Page 206.

~~I would like to go on quoting from the book, but the habit of garrulity is a [illegible] of talk (and I am talking now with the pen, as it were) is not to be controlled; as my good wife does [illegible] the ... of my paragraphs, and of [illegible] habits ... and unproductive, and ... the ... [illegible] ... life — an attempt ... [illegible] ... as it ... [illegible]~~

The poems of Rupert Brooke, ~~and~~ especially the war ~~familiar to~~ sonnets, are familiar to many people; but how many know the work of Wilfred Owen? ~~His~~ ~~[illegible]~~ Owen did not write very much, at least, his published verse ~~[illegible]~~ fills one slim volume only. I like to think of that volume going down the years ~~with~~ ~~[illegible]~~, and I believe it will be known when much present day verse, widely hailed, is forgotten. It is

(10

of the stuff of greatness — the spirit of
Every man ~~to the~~ ~~...~~ ~~...~~ ~~use~~ ~~that dominates~~ ~~to be~~ Until I had space for ~~quote~~ all that I
~~want to quote in my~~ ~~regard for such things,~~ feel impelled to say in my
~~to say about Owen~~
regard for ~~the~~ his work and the spirit that shines in it,
but alas, I am ~~...~~ of time and space, and ~~limited~~ time I shall
this article runs on. Perhaps in another Wilfred Owen,
be enabled to write a paper on the last months of the war. ~~Once~~
who was killed in the last months of the war "wangled" his
invalided for wounds earlier on, he his old infantry
way ~~back~~ back to the men of his old after Third Ypres,
company. Were there any left after him? He had written of
one wonders. ~~that~~ ~~his Greater~~ to greet the poem called Greater Love
them, in

Red lips are not so red
As the stained stones kissed by the English dead.
Kindness of wooed and wooer
Seems shame to their love pure.
O Love, your eyes lose lure
When I behold eyes blinded in my stead!

Your slender attitude
Trembles not exquisite like limbs knife-skewed,
Rolling and rolling there
Where God seems not to care;
Till the fierce love they bear
Cramps them in death's extreme decrepitude.

Your voice sings not so soft,—
Though even as wind murmuring through raftered loft,—
Your dear voice is not dear,
Gentle, and evening clear,
As theirs whom none now hear
Now earth has stopped their piteous mouths that coughed.

11

Heart, you were never hot,
Nor large, nor full like hearts made great with shot;
And though your hand be pale,
Paler are all which trail
Your cross through flame and hail;
Weep, you may weep, for you may touch them not.

And one would like to quote (buried in Rome) the present time, what Francis Thompson wrote of Keats in the essay called Shelley: "Posterity! that weeps large-sized tears, and but never a posterity that goes to Rome, and carves beautiful inscriptions ... bones the less dry for all the tears."

Forgive me if I have misquoted anyone; but my books are in Devon, and if I have quoted without (memory), moved by the sound, as of a falling phosgene gas shell, made by the quick-closing motor car in the road below.

Henry Williamson.

12/12/26

A Selection of 'Notes' re 1914 and 1915

Henry Williamson

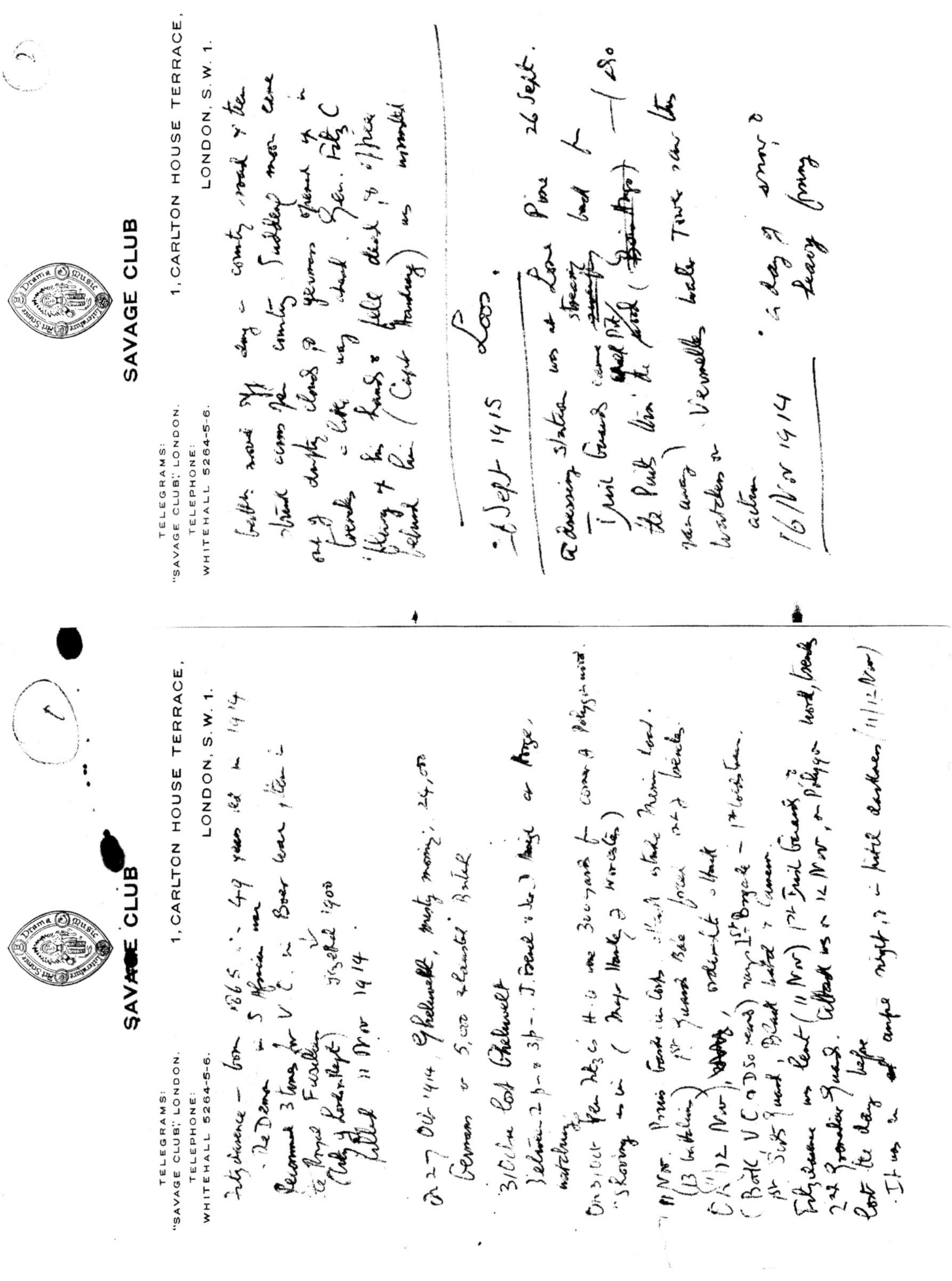

1915.

Westy speaks "Come into my funk-hole, & have a spot of old man whiskey."

Lone Tree is on 50 metre contour, about 350 yards from Br. Trenches & 50 from Germans, = 400 yds between the lines.

1st & 2nd Inf Bde were at Le Rutoire 25 Sept.

1st Bde would be getting MG stream from the Quarries beyond Breslau trench & Fritz redoubt beyond the Hulluch road, about 1 mile from Bois Carré.

Maroc is 75 metres - 70 metres up

21st Div went through Mazingarbe on morning of 25 Sept.

Re heavy rain began to fall on evening of 24th Sept & contd. all night. [Guards Div moved from S. of AIRE at 6am on 25th.

Raining at 9.30, & at 11.30 am.

& at 2pm. "incessantly" the Guards Div. moved off again, to Noeux-les-Mines. March was 16 miles. (after 4 hours 6 AM - 10 pm marching) with continuous stoppages. No traffic control. — transports of 47th, 21, & 24 Div. in the way, + Cav. Corps.

Guards reached destination at midnight.

On 26th Sept, 1st Div attack on Hulluch failed: also attacks of 21 & 24 between Hulluch & Hill 70. Also 15th Div to regain Hill 70 failed.

Gds ordered to march at 1pm on 26th to position of readiness in & rear of old Br. front line trenches between the Le Rutoire — Loos & Vermelles — Hulluch Road.

1st Div front from Northern Sap, out of German lines
to Hulluch – Vermelles Road.

Original front line was 800 yards from German.
Jumping off trenches were dug early Sept, closer to
crest of the Grenay ridge, & the German line were
not visible from front line (Germans were 157 Regiment, 400 men)
Owing to danger of M.Gs from the S. & N saps, a gap of
600 yards was left, to be bombed up from South (15th Div)

2nd Bde (under B.G. J. Pollard) was to assault on 600 yard
front from Northern Sap to Lone Tree — a CHERRY tree,
15ft high, white-blossom in May. P. Smelt bark &
so found it a cherry. <u>No leave in Sept.</u>

1st Bde between Lone Tree & Vermelles – Hulluch Road.

Wind from South enfiladed the trenches of 2nd Bde

At 6.20 am wind ~~[illegible]~~ veered back to S-west

at 6.34 am 2nd Bde (2/KRRC & 1st L.N. Lancs) went
over: enfiladed by machine guns in sap-heads 40 yards
in front of main German trench, one in N. Sap, the other South of
Lone Tree. Ger. wire was over the crest: 10 yds wide,
staked low (to be invisible). Troops lay before wire.
2nd wave lay 100 yards back behind the crest.
There were two copses in front of 1st Bde (Bois Carré and La Haie)
Saps dug to them from German line.
Gloucestershires were decimated by m.g. fire in the advance (1st Bde)
Berkshires got thro' enemy wire, and by 8 am were in German
Trench, 1200 yards from the British front. Two lone poplar trees on
Lens – La Bassée road, 500 yards N. could be seen
Some 30 1/Cameron Highlanders were <u>said</u> to have got to Hulluch, by 9.10 am.

7.45 am Brigadier Pollard (1st Bde) ordered support batt. (2 Royal Sussex) & 2 companies of the 1 Northamptonshires, in Bde reserve.

2nd assault reported successful: at 8-5 am message sent to 1 Div, "2nd Bde held up at first by Sussex have got thro' in German trenches."

So Div (1st) order 2nd Bde to "push on with all speed", with Green's Force behind & 3rd Bde, in div. reserve at Le Rutoire, to follow Green

At 9.1 am contradiction reached Div Hq that 2nd Bde (Sussex & Northamps) held up on wire south of ~~Lone~~ Lone Tree

Comm ~~Those~~ trenches were filled with wounded & gassed men coming back

at 9 am. Germans had worked north abreast of Bois Carré & were in the sap thereto.

Captured Captain Ritter of 157 Regt., & men of the (ammo. and) → 59th and 51st (drafts) "Ram out of (hand grenades" (i.e. 1st batt of 157 Regt).

Kings Liverpools & Lond. Scottish took the prisoners.

Attack, time of surrender, delivered from Hulluch on line of 1st Bde along Lens Road, made by reserve batt. of 157 Regt.

Fading light — leaden sky — could nevertheless see the straight white line of the Lens Road, & beyond it, on Hill 70, the two copses of Chalet Wood & Bois Hugo.

4.15 pm. Casualties of 2nd Bde 2224 by nightfall of 25 Sept. including Green's Force.

(2)

2nd. Guards Bde

1 Coldstream
1 Scots Guard
3 G.G.
2 Irish Gds.

} at Houchin on night of 25/26 Sept.

on 21 Sept wind was in the East.

Adv. Div H Q small house in main St of Sailly - Labourse

At 2.10 pm } reversal order, after failure of morning attacks, Guards to advance to old German front line in front of previously allotted sector.

1st. Guards Bde in cellar of Le Rutoire farm

1st + 2nd. Bdes ordered to relieve the 21st + 24th

Divisions at 1 AM of 27th Sept

Guards line from point on Lens / Bassee road 800 yds SE of Hulluch to 60 yds S-E of Lone Tree. ~~Others in~~

At 6. am of 27th 2nd Bde from Fort Glatz on NW outskirts of Loos, N along the western side of Lens - La Bassee road

Berties batt (1st. I.C.G.) was in 1st & 2nd German line north of Loos.

By 6 am the 2nd Bde (Gds) Hq from Rutoire went to Loos

Temple clears gets into position - stragglers - dead - few casualties from shelling

(3)

2 p.m 27 Sept Gds
ordered to attack Chalk Pit &
Puits No 14 Bis & Hill 70.

Chalk Pit Wood was west of
Lens - La Bassée Road, 1/2 mile
NE of Loos (M guns).

Haig wanted to stop the
attack having learned at 2.30
from Hq Fosse 8 (& Dump) was retaken by
German : but too late

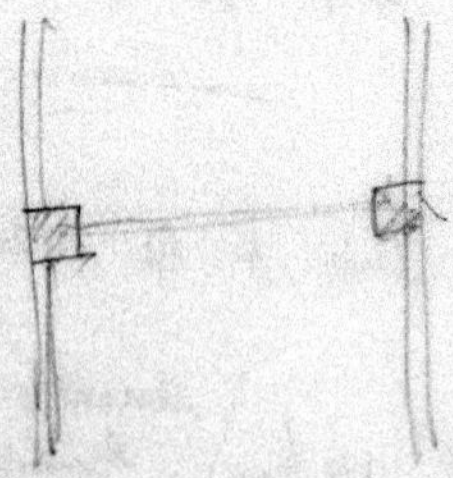

2nd Bde attack on Chalk Pit & Puits 14 bis. (tall red chimney)
before Bois Hugo.
Brig PONSONBY. (at Loos).

2nd I.G to attack Chalk Pit at 4 p.m.
Supported by 1st ~~S.G~~ C.G.

3rd G.G in support
Adv in smoke from trench S-W of Hulluch Down the slope & up.
Meanwhile
(Scots Guards in extended order doubled down the slope from Br. trenches & came under heavy shrapnel fire. Limit the Loos - Hulluch road. up the slope met a withering fire from Bois Hugo, the Keep, & the Puits (red brick buildings).
Reached Puits with 11 officers, including Lt Col Godman, casualties in the advance. A small party of entered the Puits & held on.
Meanwhile 1st C.G. supporting Irish G. fell back to
western side of Chalk Pit wood.

(2)

At nightfall of 25/26 Sept

Neither 1st nor 3rd Bde knew
that 2nd Bde & Green's force had
~~reached~~ come up: & no report reached
these generals (1st & 3rd). So they
withdrew from the Lens road, unable to dig
trenches. Their right was exposed, they
thought, not knowing that the 2nd & G. Force were
about Bois Hugo: so they retired to German
comm. trench Alley 4, running to Lone Tree
So gap of about a mile was
on left of 2nd Bde.

1st Div. never knew this
Both 2nd Bde & 1st & 3rd had reported
at 5 pm. (Rawlinson at 8.30 visited his
div. generals & was not told of any gap, &
remained ignorant of the gap all night

Extracts from Letters found on Germans during the SOMME BATTLE.

Undated. "You should have seen the recruits who were mustered this week; it was like the boys coming out of school, but they have all become soldiers; it hardly seems possible. On 24th November there is another muster in Röhrsdorf—this time for the older, untrained men, till now unfit for active service, and for those who have become unfit during the war. I don't know whether I shall have to go too, we get a special notice from the district command. I am prepared for everything—Germany's last hope."

Extract from an undated letter written by a man of the 3rd Reserve Ersatz Regiment.

"Since April 10th we have changed our position four times, the first three were quite good, a man could hope to return home again, but the one we now occupy is a bad witches' cauldron, one is glad if one gets out of it with sound limbs. On the first day I had lost hope; a T.M. bomb fell beside our dug-out, tore away the door and filled the place with dust; the six of us inside thought we were lost. As soon as we saw daylight again, we went into the front trench to watch whether any more of these projectiles were being fired, for one can see them coming in the daytime; it is worst of all at night for then they cannot be seen.

"The work here is terrible; it is unheard of what they expect us to do. On one occasion we ceased work, as we were done up; so that the Company Commander had to detail other men. No man can stand work day and night.

"I hope the cruel war is approaching its end, for one no longer has any heart for this sort of thing."

The following is an extract from a Regimental Order of 5th Bavarian Reserve Regiment (4th Bavarian Division):—

30-8-16. "I have occasion to draw attention to the following:—The demand for artillery barrage and the nervous firing of the rifles, because an unseen bomber throws a few hand grenades, reveals a state of great excitement. The result is nothing; on the contrary, it is only harmful. We waste an enormous quantity of ammunition, and when we want it, it is gone. Secondly, we damage ourselves in the eyes of the enemy. It has been constantly stated that troops have thrown an enormous quantity of hand grenades because they heard one enemy grenade exploded somewhere. I want this sort of thing stopped. It does us a lot of damage. The men must remain calm and keep their presence of mind. I count on the help of my officers and sergt.-majors. I have got the impression that a few Englishmen throwing grenades from their trenches can thoroughly frighten a crowd of Bavarians. Things must not go on like this. Why always silently acknowledge the superiority of the enemy without any reason?

"The Artillery Commander has assured me that this state of things cannot continue. Both his ammunition and guns are done for.

"Only Company Commanders may order rapid fire or volleys of hand-grenades. There are plenty of watchful Company Commanders with presence of mind. If troops open rapid fire without orders it shows lack of discipline and despicable cowardice.

"If we put an unnecessary barrage on the enemy's trenches, he retaliates, and therefore we suffer for it.

"Instead of demanding unnecessary barrage, or wasting hand grenades it is much better to do something useful; strengthen our wire entanglements, deepen our trenches, and build strong shell-proof dug-outs for the garrison.

"This state of terror on the Somme front must be dispelled, and calm must take its place."

(Signed) VON HAASY, Lt.-Col.

Extracts from letters from a man of the 119th R.I.R.

8-9-16. "We have been relieved and are resting at Inchy, near Cambrai. We have had some strenuous days, especially on the 3rd September. The English attacked our 1st and 2nd Battalions and managed to reach the third line; we were sent up to repulse them. Some of the companies of the 1st and 2nd Battalions were practically annihilated. Companies of your regiment turned up too, only after the battle was over."

153rd Regiment, Battalion Command Post. (Probably Stuff Redoubt.)

22-9-16. "In case of an attack we are not in a position to defend ourselves, much less to attack—the rifles have been dragged through the mud and are useless for shooting, all we have are bayonets and hand grenades, but I think if the "Tommies" came no one would put up a fight, the men would gladly go over to them."

180th Regiment, Machine Gun Company. (S. of Thiepval.)

26-9-16. "We relieved a Machine Gun crew who had the only entrance to their dug-out knocked in by a shell after a gas bomb had fallen in it. You can't imagine what misery this is. Our Company Commander was gassed and is now in hospital.

"The bombardment has again begun at a rate to make a man dizzy. I think we shall soon have to either get out or be taken by the English."

Thiepval. (Probably 180th Regiment.)

26-9-16. "We must reckon with the possibility of an attack at any moment and we are in a tight corner. The English now have aerial torpedoes which have a frightful effect."

From the diary of a man of the 66th Regiment (52nd Division).

"On the night of October 2nd the regiment was relieved (in the Thiepval sector); it has lost 37 officers and 1,400 men. Of the 1st Company only the ration carriers are left.

"In the afternoon we arrived in Achiet-le-Petit. Miraumont, till now untouched, is completely destroyed."

1-10-16. "We have returned to the trenches. What we most feared has happened to us. We are in the trenches near Thiepval. . . . Our company has already suffered heavy losses. We hope we shall soon be leaving this sector. There is no cover in the front line trenches; it would have been better had we never been relieved, for in Beaumont we were alright."

From a Landsturm man to a man of the 111th R.I.R.

Baden, *8-10-16.* "As regards my transfer I suppose nothing will be done. Father got a petition sent in to H.Q., but up to the present nothing has come of it. Only the farmers and the Jews can work that sort of thing, but some day the war will end; it can never go on thus, for I think all people have had enough of leading such a life. The Russians have got a proper dose this week; I think they will soon stop and make peace. If only some stop, so that we have a prospect (of peace). . . . . After the war things will be better, I fancy, and there will be enough work."

From a letter.

20-10-16. "We are again in front of Serre. It is frightful the way the 'Tommies' attack us. We are in a miserable state of mind. I hope I shall be lucky as regards my leave so that my nerves may have a chance to recover."

To a man of the 121st I.R. from his wife.

23-10-16. "One cannot think any longer of an end to the war. On the contrary we continue to make more enemies. I infer from your letter that you and Hermann are about to desert to the English and meet there. You are right to do so, so that some are left who are not 'kaput.' But how will you be treated there? It is possible that you may receive better treatment than you are getting at present; but one cannot tell. Have you arranged it with Hermann?"

From a man of "Fl. A. K. Zug 116" (Wurtt.) to a N.C.O. of the 120th R.I.R. (Wurtt.).

25-10-16. "You write that you are presumably again going into the hell on the Somme. I could have cried when I read that; why must the blood of our brave Suabians always be shed? It is abominable."

3-11-16. "Yes, we still get food, but there could be more of it. For being day and night in the open air gives you an appetite. . . . We are chased round from one bad position to another. At present we are near Thiepval, and what that means you will probably know if you follow the news in the paper. I will say only one thing, that is that we shan't recover our senses if things go on as they are."

Carpathians.

3-11-16. "You are, I suppose, released from hell now. You know what I mean, don't you? You fellows have now a better time for a few days, but we are out of one hole into another. Here all the guns are banging away. We have changed our position and have got into a God-forsaken one. We are up to our knees in water, snow and filth; and, besides that, every morning shells come over by way of a morning greeting. I really have no taste for the business now.

"I was to have a few days leave, but you know such things hang by a thread, and if that breaks, it's all over. My brother Johann is best off. He went home for ever a few days ago. I should like to do so, too. How about you? And then the Austrians blackguard us and ask us what we have come here for, and say we only want to prolong the war. They are all fools . . . it would be the same to them even if the Russians had occupied Cracow again. The chief thing for them is that the war should end."

Bremen.

22-11-16. "Our 2nd Company at the front consists now only of young recruits 18-19 years old. Unfortunately, on September 3rd, in consequence of several English attacks not a man of the 1st Battalion came back.

Extracts from a letter dated 21-11-16 and written by a man of the 25th Regiment (208th Division) at present in the North of Beaucourt:—

"It is impossible to describe how awful it is here. I should not wish my worst enemy in the hell of the Somme. It is said that we must remain here till December 2nd or 3rd; I can't conceive that we could hold out as long as that. If we were only safely out of it: every second is torture—we all feel like that. The mud here is worse than in Galicia, and anyhow, war there is child's play to this."

No. 4 Advanced Section. A.P. & S.S., 251. 38000, 4/17.

The Orders for the Attack on the Hindenburg Line May 1917 – Henry Williamson's own copy

62ND DIVISION.

ORDER OF THE DAY.

As the Division will shortly be going into action to take part in its first great battle, the Divisional Commander desires to assure all ranks of his complete confidence in their ability to defeat the German troops opposed to them.

That the 62nd (West Riding) Division will maintain its reputation for staunchness and grit - qualities for which Yorkshiremen have ever been famed - that they will gain all objectives and hold them against the most determined counter-attacks, is the firm conviction of the General Officer who is proud to be their Commander.

Major General.
Commanding 62nd (West Riding) Division.

May 1st 1917.

S E C R E T. COPY NO. 10

62ND. DIV[redacted]N ORDER NO. 36. 13.4.17.

REF:- Maps 51.B.S.W.)
57.C.N.W.) 1/20,000.

1. [redacted], The attack on the HINDENBURG LINE, ordered in 62nd.Division Order No. 31 of 8.4.17, will take place on a date (not before April 16th.) and at an hour to be notified later, unless the enemy withdraw previously on account of the attack of the Third Army.

2. In addition to the Objectives laid down in the above Order, the 62nd.Division will be responsible for the capture of BULLECOURT. This will be carried out by the 185th. Infantry Brigade, less 1 Battalion.
The 2nd.Australian Division will attack on the right of the 185th. Infantry Brigade -- boundaries as shown on the attached sketch.

3. The Objectives, frontages and boundaries of the 186th. and 187th. Infantry Brigades will be as in 62nd.Division Order No.31.
1 Battalion of the 185th. Infantry Brigade will be placed at the disposal of G.O.C. 186th. Infantry Brigade to hold the 2nd. Objective and release a battalion 186th. Infantry Brigade to move forward to the 3rd. Objective.

4. The advance from the 1st. Objective to the 2nd. Objective will commence at Zero plus 1 hour and 15 minutes; the advance from the 2nd. Objective to the 3rd. Objective will commence at Zero plus 2 hours and 15 minutes. The hours mentioned in paras. 3, 7 and 8 of 62nd.Division Order No. 31 will be amended accordingly.

5. Battalions of 185th. Infantry Brigade attacking BULLECOURT will jump off at 2 minutes before Zero hour and will advance at the rate of 100 yards in 2 minutes to the 1st. Objective.

6. 186th. and 187th. Infantry Brigades will form up under cover of their own posts.
The 185th. Infantry Brigade will form up under cover of the posts of 186th. Infantry Brigade which cover the frontage of their attack, and will form up on the railway line in U.27.d. and the road running North in U.27.d, U.27.c. and U.27.a.
The posts held by the 187th. Infantry Brigade West of U.20.a.4.0. will be taken over by a battalion of the 7th.Division on the evening of the 14th.April -- arrangements to be made direct between 187th. Infantry Brigade and 7th.Division.

7. The formations and method of attack will be as laid down in 62nd.Division Order No.31, with the exception that the strong bombing party ordered to be pushed Eastwards down the German trench from U.21.d.6.6. by the 186th. Infantry Brigade, and the 2 Companies 'D' Battalion of the 186th. Infantry Brigade ordered to 'mop' up the Western half of the village of BULLECOURT, are cancelled.
The right attacking battalion of the 186th. Infantry Brigade will however have parties detailed :-
(a) To push into BULLECOURT from the West, and
(b) To bomb down the trench N. of the village in the event of the 185th. Infantry Brigade failing to reach that trench before the barrage lifts.

8. 185th.Infantry Brigade will detail a special bombing party to deal with the German trench on the East of the village in U.28.a.
185th. Infantry Brigade will not advance beyond the trench North of BULLECOURT running from U.21.d.6.6. to U.22.c.9.3.
After leaving the 1st. Objective, the 186th. Infantry Brigade will therefore prolong their right and be responsible for gaining and maintaining touch with the 2nd. Australian Division, special attention being paid to the Sunken Roads running N.E. in U.22.

where/

where strong parties of the enemy are liable to be met with.

9. In place of the strong battle patrols mentioned in para. 8 of Division Order No. 31, 1 Battalion of the 186th. Infantry Brigade and 2 Companies of the 187th. Infantry Brigade will push forward at Zero hour plus 2 hours and 15 minutes under an artillery barrage to the 3rd. Objective.

10. Amended artillery programme will be issued later.

11. 1 Brigade of the 7th. Division will be in Reserve in the valley North West of MORY, in place of 185th. Infantry Brigade.

12. Orders re Tanks will be issued later.

13. LIAISON.

Liaison Officers will be detailed between :-

62nd. Divisional Headquarters and 2nd. Australian Division.
185th. Infantry Brigade and Left Brigade 2nd. Australian Division.
Right Battalion 185th. Infantry Brigade and Left Battalion 2nd. Australian Division.

These Officers will keep their own units informed of the progress of the Units to which they are attached.

14. Watches will be synchronised at 12 noon, and 5 p.m. on 'Y' day.

15. REPORT CENTRES.

Divisional Report Centre :--	B.13.b.2.3.
185th. Infantry Brigade 186th. Infantry Brigade. 187th. Infantry Brigade	B.17.a.8.7.

16. With the above exceptions 62nd. Division Order No. 31. and Instructions for attack on the HINDENBURG LINE will hold good.

17. ACKNOWLEDGE.

Issued at 11 pm.

G. Hore-Ruthven.
Lieut. Colonel,
General Staff, 62nd. Division.

Copies to:-

1 A.D.C. for G.O.C.
2 G.S.O.1.
3-5 'G'
6 'Q'
7 G.O.C.R.A.
8 C.R.E.
x 9-10 185th. Inf: Bde.
x 11-12 186th. do
x 13-14 187th. do
15 Signals
16 A.D.M.S.
17 A.P.M.
18 201st. M.G. Coy.
19 208th. M.G. Coy.
20 212th. M.G. Coy.
21 213th. M.G. Coy.
22-23 V. Corps
24 V. Corps 'Q'
25 V Corps H.A.
26 7th. Divn.
27 Anzac Corps
x 28 2nd. Aust. Divn.
29 21st. Divn.
30 4th. Cav. Divn.
31 No. 11 Coy. H. Batt. M.G. Coy.
32 P. Special Coy. R.E.
33 V Corps M.G. Officer
34 V Corps Cav. Regt.

x Sketch attached.

SECRET.

INSTRUCTIONS FOR ATTACK ON THE HINDENBURG LINE NO.5.

TANKS.

1. 6 Tanks will assist the 62nd Division in the attack on the HINDENBURG LINE.

2. Their tasks will be allotted as follows :-

1st OBJECTIVE.

One pair will assist in the capture of BULLECOURT and trenches on the East and North of that village, dealing with any strong points that may be holding out.

One pair will be responsible for trenches West of BULLECOURT as far as U.21.a.9.5.

One pair will be responsible for the trench system from U.21.a.9.5. to the strong point at U.20.b. inclusive.

2nd OBJECTIVE.

When the Infantry move forward tanks will advance conforming to the barrage.

One pair will be responsible for SUNKEN ROAD running North through U.21.a.2.8 and U.15.c.

One pair will be responsible for trench running through U.21.a.9.5. - U.15.d.5.0 - U.15.d.9.4, and any adjacent strong points.

One pair will assist the Infantry in U.22.c and U.22.a.

3. All Tanks will assist in the capture of the 2nd Objective, each Tank operating in its allotted area.

4. The Tanks will follow the Infantry as closely as possible, but the Infantry will not wait for the Tanks.

5. ACKNOWLEDGE.

Lieut-Colonel.
General Staff 62nd Division.

20.4.1917.

Copies to :-

A.D.C. for G.O.C.
G.S.O. 1
"Q"
G.O.C.R.A.
C.R.E.
185th Brigade.
186th Brigade.
187th Brigade.
Signals.
201st M.G.Coy.
208th M.G.Coy.
212th M.G.Coy.
213th M.G.Coy.

V Corps (2)
V Corps H.A.
7th Divn.
Anzac Corps.
2nd Aust. Divn.
33rd Divn.
V Corps Cav. Regt.
War Diary (2)

CONFIDENTIAL: NOT TO BE ISSUED TO COMMANDERS OF LOWER RANK THAN BATTALION, BATTERY AND FIELD COMPANY COMMANDERS, AND NOT TO BE TAKEN INTO FRONT LINE TRENCHES.

18/3/17. V CORPS SUMMARY OF INTELLIGENCE. No.205.

PART I.

INFORMATION FROM OUR OWN FRONT.

1. OPERATIONS.

The enemy continued his withdrawal throughout the night of the 17/18th March, evacuating COURCELLES, DOUCHY, AYETTE, GOMIECOURT, MOYENNEVILLE and HAMELINCOURT and ERVILLERS. These villages are now occupied by our troops.

The Corps on our right have extended their line to FREMICOURT, BEUGNATRE, FAVREUIL, SAPIGNIES and are pushing patrols forward which have now reached MORY.

The Corps on our left is now in occupation of ADINFER WOOD, ADINFER, HENDECOURT, RANSART, BLAIREVILLE and FICHEUX.

In all these operations practically no opposition was met with from the enemy.

For our approximate line see attached map.

2. ENEMY DISPOSITIONS.

Owing to the rapidity of the enemy's retreat, it has been difficult to keep touch. At the present moment there is no information to hand of the dispositions of his main troops, but his nearest line is part of the HINDENBURG system running in a south-easterly direction East of St.MARTIN SUR COJEUL and CROISILLES through BULLECOURT.

Reports have been received that enemy posts are situated in a crater in front of ST.LEGER at B.3.b. and also in ECOUST ST.MEIN.

Hostile cavalry patrols have also been seen on the road between ERVILLERS and ST.LEGER and S.W. of ECOUST ST.MEIN in C.7 and 8.

3. IDENTIFICATIONS.

(a) A very severely wounded prisoner of the 3rd Coy.55th R.I.R. (220th Division) was taken at QUESNOY FARM early this morning. He stated that his company left their normal sector near RANSART for BOIRY ST.MARTIN early last night. He, however, fell out and lost his way and wandered about until he was wounded and found by our troops near QUESNOY FARM.

From his statements, it appears that the 220th Division came into the RANSART area on 28th February. He was ignorant of the order of battle, but said the 207th R.I.R. was on his left.

As the prisoner was in a dying condition and half unconscious from morphia, his statements should be taken with reserve.

(b) Two unwounded prisoners of the 55th R.I.R.(220th Div.) have been captured at COURCELLES.

At the time of writing these prisoners have not yet been examined.

4. ...

4. ENEMY'S WITHDRAWAL PRECAUTIONS.

(a) Fires are reported this afternoon in :-
BOIRY BECQUERELLE.
BOIRY ST.MARTIN
BOISLEUX ST.MARC
VAULX
VRAUCOURT
MOREUIL
QUEANT
ST.LEGER
CROISILLES.
and many other fires were observed in villages further East.
(b) It appears from observers' reports that practically all cross-roads, level crossings, entrances to and exits from villages have been blown up. On several roads trees have been cut down to block the roads. With the exception of the above, the roads are in good condition. For position of the above mentioned obstacles, see attached map.
(c) The rails of the Railway from ARRAS - ACHIET-le-GRAND - BAPAUME have been torn from the sleepers.

5. ARTILLERY.

(a) Our Artillery: Our artillery supported the advance of our infantry and shelled the enemy's roads and tracks and usual targets.
(b) Enemy's activity: Enemy's artillery activity has been practically nil. Shortly after midnight 17/18th inst., the southern outskirts of BUCQUOY were shelled with 150 mm.
Our Cavalry report that the northern exit of HAMELINCOURT was shelled with gas shells and the CROISILLES - HAMELINCOURT road at A.6.c.2.5 with long range shrapnel.

6. CAPTURED DOCUMENT.

Regimental Order of 77th R.I.R.
(i) The band will proceed on the 13/3/17 to MARQUION (6 miles W. of CAMBRAI) and will be attached to the Infantry Pioneer Company. They will work on the new position.
(ii) The Regimental Post Office should be transferred by rail from ST.LEGER to MARQUION and from here further by road to SAINS LES MARQUIONS, so long as the Field Post Office remains in ST.LEGER.

=============

PART II.

INFORMATION FROM OTHER SOURCES.

A. PRECAUTIONS FOR WITHDRAWAL.

A prisoner captured by the Army on our right states that orders were given by the Germans to poison wells. The well at BARLEUX was examined and found to be poisoned with arsenic.
The Army on our left report working parties on the HINDENBURG LINE.
All villages west of this line are in flames.

ST. LEGER.

(Reference 1/20,000 sheets 57c N.W. and 51b S.W.).

---

1. General.

(a) ST.LEGER, a village of 171 houses, stands in a valley, that of the Upper SENSEE, running from south-west to north-east. There is high ground north and south of the village. In the village itself the ground rises from north to south and the hill is steep. All villages in the neighbourhood except CROISILLES are hidden, but from the high ground south of the village there is a wide view in every direction.

(b) The neighbourhood of the village and the village itself are particularly well wooded. There are large trees along the roads at all the exits from the village, along the banks of the stream and in the orchards and pastures surrounding the village. The gardens are enclosed by thick hedges and fences. Half the village area consists of the large chateau park which is well wooded.

2. Woods.

Apart from the plantations in the immediate neighbourhood of the village, there are numerous small copses in the open country beyond. These are intended to serve as cover for partridges and are all shown on the 1/20,000 maps of the area.

3. Watercourse.

The SENSEE at this point is dry except as the result of heavy rain. It is from 6 to 8 feet wide, and its banks are about 4 feet deep and not abrupt. The road bridges over the watercourse marked on the map are all of brick.

4. Water Supply.

There is one large pond on the road to ERVILLERS. There are 50 wells, and the average depth of water level is 40 feet.

5. Railway.

ST.LEGER is on the BOISLEUX-MARQUION railway. The track is broad gauge and single. There is a "Halte" about T 28 central with a siding and a loop line. East of the station the line is embanked for about 1,000 yards; through the village it is level, from T 28 a 40 to T 27 b 71 it is embanked, and from this point to T 27 a 19 it is in a fairly deep cutting.

6. Roads.

The roads are of the usual type; sunken at the exits of the village; slightly sunken or level in the open country. There is a deep cutting on the road at the southern exit from the village in B 4 b and d (the banks are said to be 20 feet high). Practically every road is lined with trees as it leaves the village, those to VAULX-VRAUCOURT and MAISON ROUGE FARM for a considerable distance.

The CROISILLES road passes under the railway.

The ECOUST and VAULX-VRAUCOURT roads are unmetalled.

7. Buildings.

By far the most important building is the chateau. There are a few large brick farms and a brick sugar factory, but most of the houses are small two storeyed farms, built of brick and torchis. There are cellars to almost every house, the only important ones being those under the chateau and the factory. JUDAS FARM, T 27 a 10, and ST.LEGER Mill T 21 d 92 are important buildings away from the village.

8.

8. Underground passages.
There is said to be an underground gallery, one kilometre long, at ST.LEGER. It is rather remarkable that although it is at least 70 feet below the surface, the soil of the passages and rooms is of beaten clay. In 1885, during the digging of a well, one of the streets of this underground village was discovered, 26 rooms and stables were counted, and there were 5 vent holes that had provided ventilation and exits for the passage of smoke, for some of the rooms had fire places. These ventilations had, however, collapsed. The street was only 3 feet wide, the rooms were about 8 feet high by 9 feet square and the doors 6 feet high. The entrance discovered was in the garden of the chateau.

9. Quarry.
The quarry shown on the map at T 28 a 31 is reported to be from 15 to 20 feet deep.

10. Obstacles.
None of the various terraces marked on the 1/20,000 map, north-west and south-east of ST.LEGER are high nor do they present a serious obstacle.

11. Soil.
The soil of the village and of the whole valley is chalk, except that the bed of the stream is sandy. On the hills north and south of the village the surface soil is clay.

12. Present Military Organization.
Up to the present there are no signs of any trenches having been dug near ST.LEGER and the village appears to be quite undefended. The village has been consistently used as rest billets and for a long time there was a Divisional Headquarters in the chateau.

13. Population.
784 before the war. Now all evacuated.

List of important buildings.

T 28 d 22.	Chateau standing in a large wooded park. There is a garden between the chateau and the village street. Between this garden and the park there is a railing. The house itself is old and strong, with thick stone walls. Under the house there are large cellars and vaults. Attached to the chateau there are good stables and farm buildings.
? B 4 b 6280.	Church: a large building with a tall belfry.
T 28 c 86.	Sugar factory standing at the bottom of the hill. It is not large but is strongly built with good cellars and several large sheds.
T 28 c 7054.	Two storeyed brick house.
T 28 c 8846.	Large and strong farm.
T 27 a 10.	JUDAS FARM: isolated, astride the BOYELLES road. The buildings north of the road are strongly built and have thick walls. The cellars are 13 feet below the surface and divided into four chambers: they are vaulted with masonry. There is one entrance in the yard and one in the house. There is a pigeon loft 30 feet high from which there is a wide view. There is reported to be an underground gallery beneath the farm and road, possibly connected with the cellars.
T 21 d 92.	Strong stone windmill on the BOIRY road: stands high and is an excellent O.P.

A. <u>GERMAN BACK LINES OF DEFENCE.</u> (From G.H.Q.Summary).

(a) <u>HINDENBURG LINE.</u>

A deserter, who had worked for some time on the HINDENBURG line near CAMBRAI, gave the following information:-

(a) All dug-outs are made of concrete with head cover of 4 to 5 metres thickness.
(b) Trenches are unrevetted but well built.
(c) No specially built machine gun emplacements had been made.
(d) Concrete observation posts with about 5 metres head cover, and a periscope protected by steel plates, had been made.
(e) The wire in front of St.QUENTIN was 15 to 20 yards deep.

(b) Air reconnaissance yesterday morning confirms the line of trenches previously reported by refugees from CANTIN past ARLEUX to MARQUION. Just north of MARQUION the line bends off to the west, passing just N. of BARALLE. A continuation beyond this point could not be observed.

Those portions of line which were observed are very strongly wired, and consist in most places of both front and support trenches.

(Sgd) S.S.HILL-DILLON, Capt.,G.S.,
for B.G.,G.S.,
V Corps.

STOP PRESS

Fred Crawford's long awaited book on the controversy surrounding Richard Aldington and T.E. Lawrence arrived after this issue of the HWSJ had been typeset. Thus there is no room for a full review but at least it can be drawn to your attention *pro tem*.

Fred D. Crawford, RICHARD ALDINGTON AND LAWRENCE OF ARABIA: A Cautionary Tale. Southern Illinois University Press, USA, 1998. ISBN 0-8093-2166-1.
This book examines the extraordinary arena in which the combatants were Richard Aldington and his (then) sensational work *Lawrence of Arabia: A Biographical Enquiry* (Collins, 1955) versus a group ostensibly led by B.H. Liddell-Hart and A.W. Lawrence (TE's brother and executor). In trying to protect TEL this group ('The Lawrence Bureau') went to great lengths to try to suppress Aldington's book in which he sought to clarify previous conceptions about TEL's life, particularly the mystery surrounding his birth and his role in the Arab campaign in the First World War. When their ploy failed (although the book was highly edited by result) they then tried to damage Aldington's reputation so that the book would not be taken seriously. Prof. Crawford's book gives a clear and objective discussion of the total scenario – in which Henry Williamson played a part (*see* Anne Williamson, 'The Genius of Friendship', Pt 1 'T.E. Lawrence', HWSJ, no. 27, March 1993, pp 18-35; Pt 2 'Richard Aldington', HWSJ no. 18, Sept. 1993, pp 7-21). Crawford's 'Cautionary Tale' illuminates the problems faced by one biographer in discovering the truth – and warns us that similar situations still exist. It is appallingly easy for truth to be suppressed or twisted to present a false picture. We know Henry Williamson suffered (and still suffers) from the same syndrome.

Food Shortage at Home: 1917

Note made January 1956.
I found out only in 1955 that Kearling, of A. Fox & Peter, was actually a son of Devonport – real name Kearley.
(=CURLING)

No. 67.

Ministry of Food,
Grosvenor House, W. 1.

ON HIS MAJESTY'S SERVICE.

I wish to appeal for the immediate help of every man, woman and child in my effort to reduce the consumption of bread.

We must all eat less food; especially we must all eat less bread and none of it must be wasted. The enemy is trying to take away our daily bread. He is sinking our wheat ships. If he succeeds in starving us our soldiers will have died in vain.

In the interests of the country, I call upon you all to deny yourselves, and so loyally to bridge over the anxious days between now and the harvest. Every man must deny himself; every mother, for she is the mistress of the home, must see that her family makes its own sacrifice and that not a crust or crumb is wasted.

By a strict care of our daily bread we can best help the men who are gallantly fighting on sea and land to achieve victory, and so share with them the joys of the peace which will follow.

No true citizen, no patriotic man or woman will fail the country in this hour of need.

I ask all the members of your household to pledge themselves to respond to the King's recent Appeal for economy and frugality and to wear the purple ribbon as a token.

Devonport

29th May, 1917.

Food Controller.

Remember Hetty's worries about food shortages.

TRUTHFUL POEM

BY AN

EX - SERVICE MAN

Written by

UNEMPLOYED

Ex-Soldier

This poem printed on a folded sheet reminds us of the plight of the ordinary soldier on his return home after the war to 'a land fit for heroes', and epitomises Henry's own thoughts.

T'was in the month of August, in the year Nineteen-Fourteen,
Our land was Plunged in horror, the greatest ever seen,
It came quite unexpected, we were startled with dismay,
To learn old England was at war with cruel Germany.

" England expects " the call had come to every honest man,
To guard her from invasion we answered her command,
To fight the cause of justice, of freedom and of Right,
We rallied round the Union Jack, opposed to German might.

Our Mothers, Wives, and Sweethearts bade us their last good-bye,
And sent us forth to distant lands to conquer or to die,
Their hearts were full of sadness, their eyes with tears of sorrow,
And prayed to the Almighty to protect us on the morrow.

We gave up all our happiness, we left our peaceful homes and
All the friends we loved so dear to sail across the foam,
Good occupations cast aside our country to defend,
With hope and courage in our hearts, fought to the bitter end.

Thro' all those long and weary days we suffered, aye, with pain
To keep you safe within your shores we'd do the same again,
We were heroes while it lasted, but now the battle's o'er
For the " Services we rendered " we beg from door to door.

If war broke out to-morrow you would say " Here is your gun "
" Go back and shed your blood for us till victory is won "
Oh ! " why are ye so selfish " give us this day our daily bread
Or the situations promised us before our blood was shed.

What of our poor old mothers, our sisters, and our wives
Who gave us up to battle for their freedom and their lives.
To-day they are in misery and their hearts and minds are sore
Depending on we creatures to keep the wolf away from the door.

If we were yet to fight for you and keep you safe and sound
Nestling in your feather bed while we lay on the ground,
With shot and shell around us along the bloody front,
Now the tide of war is o'er—Will you help us bear the brunt ?

To-day our hearts are full of woe our heads are bent in shame,
We are lying in the gutter with nothing but a name,
Drawing pictures on the pavement and the organ also grind
To earn an honest penny from the sympathetic kind.

What of the little children, shall they suffer in vain ;
Will ye help to feed and clothe them, their Daddies now are slain,
You surely cant deny us " according to the creed "
We appeal for some assistance for those who are in need.

A word to you Employers " give us something we can do,"
Stretch forth your helping hand, situations now are few,
Bannish all the " slackers " who then didn't care a " jot "
They hid in " safety while we—the Heroes fought."

Our pensions have been taken on what we can depend
Remember the old adage " It is ne'er too late too mend "
Give it small, but often, you will earn a just reward
Blessings good will come your way, we will thank the Lord.

Don't be selfish or hard-hearted, open up your heart to-day,
Answer now a call of mercy, help a wanderer on his way,
Lift us out of our misfortune now the roar of cannon cease
And the Saviour He will guide you to His Heavenly peace.

Honeymoon 1925: Some Postcards from the Battlefields

To: Mrs Williamson, 11 Eastern Road
'21.5.25. We arrived here last night and depart today for Albert, whence we start to walk, . . . Goodbye, it is lovely weather, but very hot with heavy packs. Love to all, H. W. W.'

To: F. Hibbert, Landcross, N. Devon.
'May 28 1925. Arras. We walked many miles here yesterday, and have now taken about 2 hrs to get ½ mile! We cannot be bothered to go on – we are sitting in a cornfield just outside Arras.'

To: W.L. Williamson, 13 Old Broad St. 'Comparatively untouched, this part! HW. 1.6.25.'

To: Mrs Williamson, 11 Eastern Road.
'Here 1.6.25. Even with all this the Bosches were untouched, mostly, in their concrete m.g. emplacements. HW.'

Chyebassa Reunion 1926

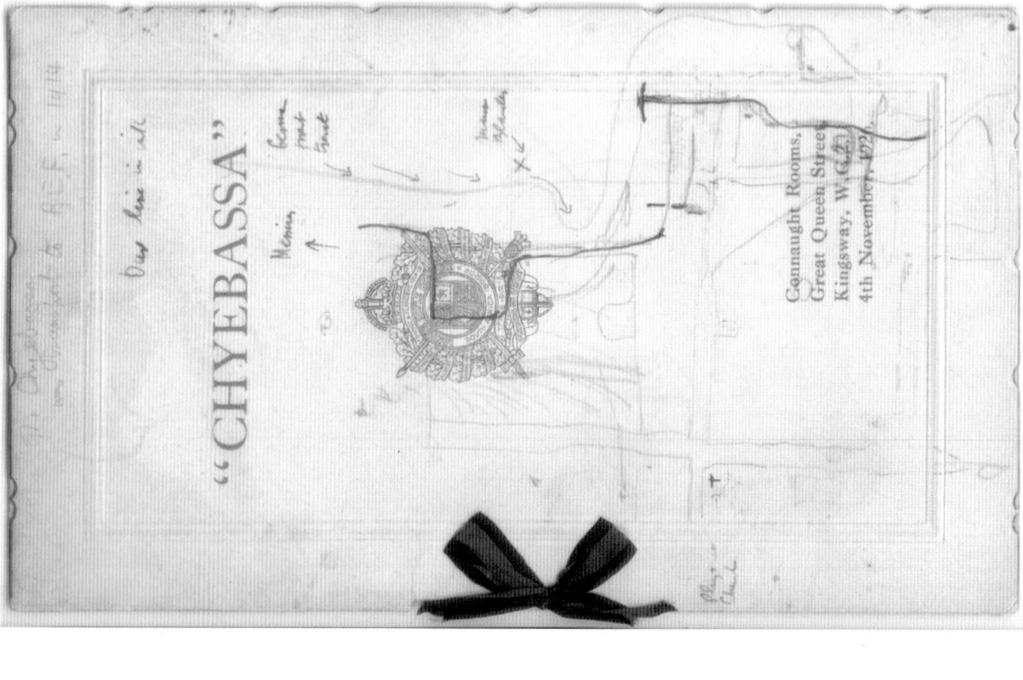

The Chyebassa *Reunion dinner, 4 November 1926, with map sketched by Lt G.E.S. Fursdon.*

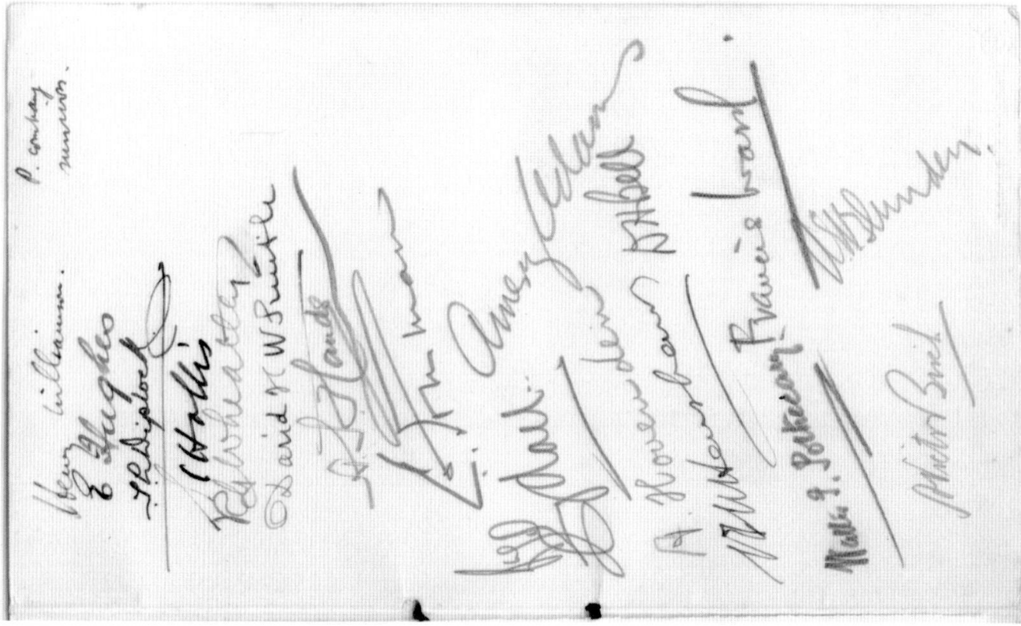

Signatures from 'P' Company survivors from inside the back cover.

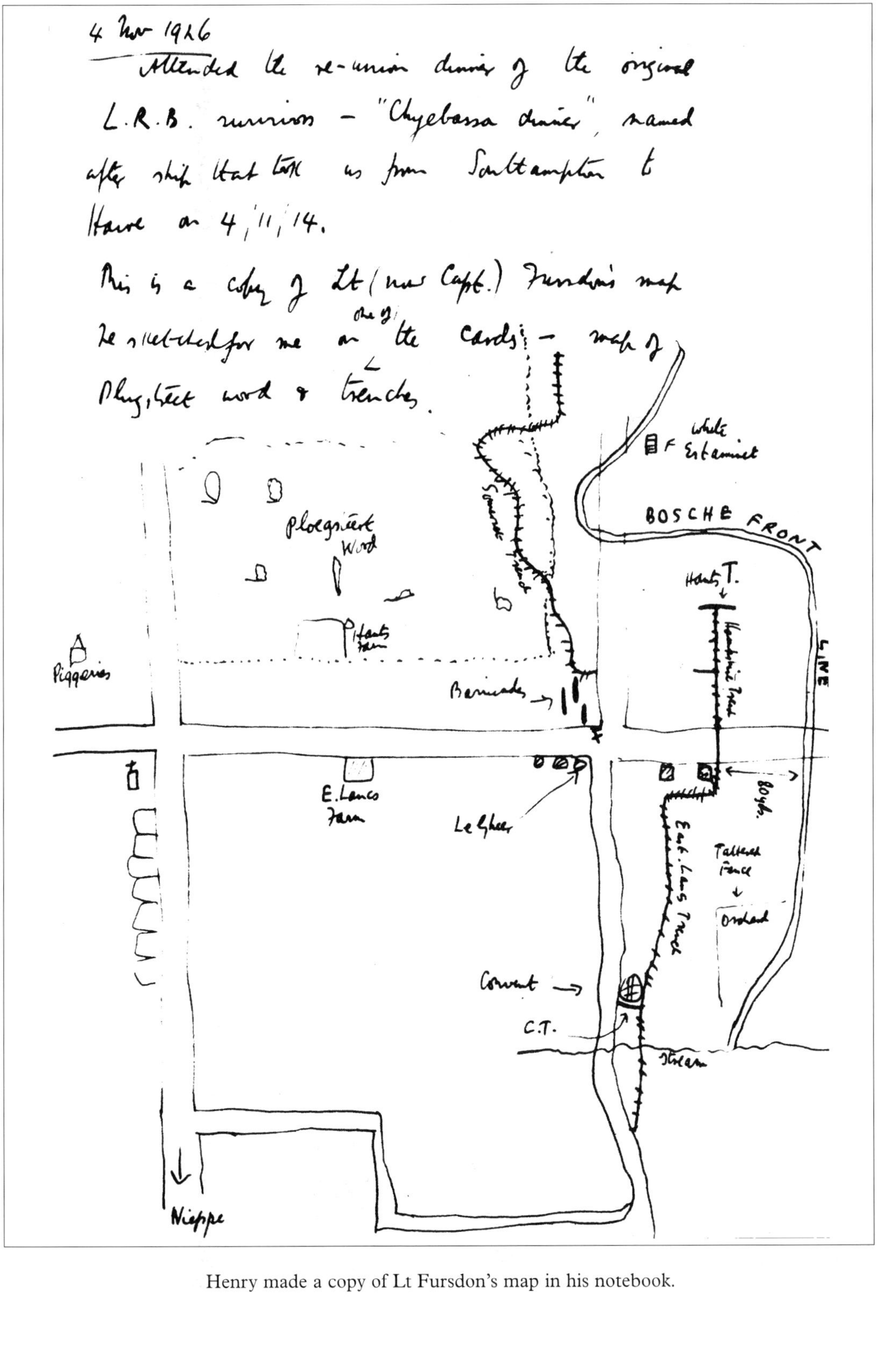
4 Nov 1926
Attended the re-union dinner of the original L.R.B. survivors – "Chyebassa dinner", named after ship that took us from Southampton to Havre on 4/11/14.
This is a copy of Lt (now Capt.) Fursdon's map he sketched for me on one of the cards – map of Plugstreet wood & trenches.
White Estaminet
BOSCHE FRONT LINE
Ploegsteert Wood
Hants T.
Hants Farm
Piggeries
Barricades
E. Lancs Farm
Le Gheer
80 yds.
East Lancs Trench
Tattered Fence
Orchard
Convent
C.T.
Stream
Nieppe

Henry made a copy of Lt Fursdon's map in his notebook.

And This Was Ypres – 1927 Visit

WEDNESDAY, THE DAILY EXPRESS, JULY 20, 1927.

AND THIS WAS YPRES.

ROAD MANY THOUSANDS WILL REMEMBER.

VLAMERTINGHE.

By HENRY WILLIAMSON.

This is the first of a series of articles by an ex-soldier, in which he describes a tour of the battlefields.

HUNDREDS of thousands of men remember the road from Poperinghe to Ypres. Its straightness begins between two long lines of houses, with tram rails laid in the right side of the road. Where the houses end the pavé ends also, and straight-boled elm trees grow at the grassy edges, above the ditches on either side.

Mr. H. Williamson.

The road lies on a raised causeway, above meadows and fields of flax, corn, and hops, stretching away on either side. Past the station the archery target, with its thatched pavilion, still stands on the left of the road, a tall green stalk like a grasshopper's leg and many-clawed foot.

Twenty-five minutes' march out of Poperinghe we saw Kemmel Hill, blue in the distance. It was captured by the enemy during his last great northern drive in April 1918, and thereafter invisible to our troops on the road. To-day you can see the rusty wires which supported the wire nets strung with coloured camouflage rags still dangling from the elms.

This country road was the main traffic artery to the Salient, and a perilous way when the enemy sat up on Kemmel Hill with his telescopes and telephones connected with his long-range batteries. It was more crowded at night than is the Strand to-day during the "rush hours"—marching men, guns, strings of pack mules, wagons, motor-cars, lorries—all congested in the darkness.

Whenever a lorry engine stopped, and failed to restart after half a dozen swings of the handle, it was pushed by scores of hands, and tipped over into the ditch. Shell-holes in the road were filled with the ruins of shattered wagons, and perhaps pieces of horse and mule, and hastily covered with earth. Then on again, thousands of tons of material, animate and inanimate, bumping, tramping, jolting forward towards the Salient. To-day every tall elm by the roadside bears its traffic scars, axle-high, from the hubs of lurching lorry and wagon.

Little trees as thick as a man's wrist grow in the gaps between the scarred forefathers of the wayside, and their roots push into the darkness of old, unnamed horse graves. The fields are beautiful with wind-stroked corn; and in the greener fields families of peasants on hands and knees crawl in line, picking out the weeds from among the ruffled flax.

Larks sing in the sky, as they have sung during all the years, and now we may share in their joyous song of freedom. Their nests are in the tussocks of meadow grass, in the slight hollows that make most of the visible ground uneven and undulating, where once shells fell—and men among them.

* * *

We walked on, alert for signs of war. We came to a red village; red brick walls, red tiled roofs, all new. At the beginning of the village stood an old, grey cement tower, like the stump of an inferior lighthouse. "Four Toes," my companion, leaned on his stick opposite this old mill-house, and said, "That was a casualty clearing station in '17. I had my arm dressed there when the splinter of an anti-tank bullet had given me a 'Blighty' one."

He stared at the mill-house, and said: "I remember So-and-so, a distinguished politician, coming up and giving the walking wounded gold-tipped cigarettes as we stood outside in the drizzle.

"He asked me how the war was going. Being out of it, with visions of going home, we said, 'Fine.' Were we keen to get back, and finish the job? 'Yes, sir.' I remember reading in the papers, a few days afterwards, his eulogy on the optimism and enthusiasm of the soldiers in the Passchendaele battles."

"Four Toes" laughed quietly. "For the good of his soul, for he was an idealist, with a wide popular appeal with words, I should have liked that politician to have come with us when 'Jerry' was crumping the tanks going up to the jumping-off points the night before the battle for Poelcapelle.

"He would have heard authentic expressions of the wounded then. The leading tank was ditched in a shell-crater, the second was on fire. Salvoes of five-nines were bursting all around. The road was a foot deep in thin watery mud, and strewn with shattered wagons and horses, drowned men, and wounded who had bled to death, covered with a hundredweight of sticking clay.

"We tried to go back the way we had come, down the road to St. Julien again, but the last tank of the column was ditched also. The ground on either side of the road was churned and rechurned six feet deep with shell holes. My tank had a direct hit, but I managed to get out with one of the crew.

"Outside, it was like standing in the middle of the flame of an immense Primus stove. Wounded infantry, going up to the tape-lines for the attack at dawn on the morrow, were crawling round the tanks, at their last gasp, seeking cover."

One small bit of Vlamertinghe remains as it was. By the first bend of the road inside the village, just before the church, stands an iron Calvary out of a grassy mound. The figure of Jesus rusts in the sunlight, the left foot broken off, the right ankle fractured. A few yards away stands the village war memorial, the figures of a soldier and a nurse cast in concrete. The memorial is already falling apart, owing to faulty erection, and is held together by iron wire.

In the churchyard tall iron crosses, factory-made, have been put up on the graves of the ancient dead, some of them more than a century old. Inside the church one sees the same lifeless spirit of materialism. The walls are decorated with stencilled patterns, hundreds repeated in each long line, the hammers and pincers, the crown of thorns and nails. The wall sculptures of Biblical scenes, cast out of a mould, are without inspiration and gaudily coloured.

In Vlamertinghe was a sad sight—a little chaffinch in a tiny wooden cage, set with a few bars in a space about two inches square. It was hopping up, hopping down, hopping up, hopping down, as quickly as you read it. They had blinded its eyes with a needle—to make it sing better.

I, who am free, know what that tiny brother was feeling, but I did not know what to do about it.

We walked on, out of Vlamertinghe.

A remarkable photograph, taken in 1918, of St. Pierre Church, Ypres, its crucifix untouched by shell-fire.

The Toc H Talbot House Chapel at Poperinghe, originally a hop-loft. (Postcard in Henry Williamson's archive reproduced with the kind permission of Toc H.) The original postcard is in colour, showing dark red mantle and backcloth, with deep green curtain drapes.

THE DAILY EXPRESS.

—AND THIS WAS YPRES.—II.

"GOLDFISH" CHATEAU MYSTERY.

CLEAN, NEW CITY.

By HENRY WILLIAMSON.

This is the second of a series of articles by an ex-soldier, describing a tour of the battlefields.

THE road leading out of Vlamertinghe towards Ypres makes a long but slight S bend. It is in full view of the Wytschaete ridge, which lies forward on the right. Old rusty camouflage-support wires are still to be seen dangling on the elms at the bend. Very soon there are no trees left, all having been topped, splintered, flaked, and finally thrown, by gunfire.

"Whitesheet" ridge is six miles distant as the airplane flies; but officer-eyesight, aided by powerful telescopes, directed through ground-level slits in certain concrete "pill-boxes," could see the dust raised by wheels and feet.

Guttural words into the telephone: a few seconds, and the dull thuds of guns behind the ridge: a few more seconds, and the bursts of shells observed on the distant road. No wonder it was necessary to take Whitesheet ridge before the great attacks of '17 could be prepared.

There used to stand an upturned gas-cylinder by the railway level-crossing between Vlamertinghe and Ypres. There was also a policeman there, night and day. "Box respirators at the alert!" You felt you were done for after passing that place.

"I shan't come back this time," one or another of the boys used to say. "Garn, don't get the —— wind up, chum," said others. "Ah, I shall be pushing up daisies soon." "What you think Wipers is, a —— park with flower gardins? There ain't no —— daisies left to push up."

DIVISIONAL H.Q.

A hundred yards to the left of the road just before the level-crossing, stands "Goldfish" chateau. Why was it never knocked down by shell-fire? It was a divisional headquarters throughout the war, and advanced G.H.Q. during the First Ypres.

It was said by German prisoners that General von Bissing, who lived in the place for three days during the German sweep forward in '14, liked it so much that he decided to take it after the war as part of his "blood money." Anyhow, it was hardly touched, even by shrapnel, although some of the goldfish in the horseshoe-shaped pond around it were occasionally seen floating on their sides.

Peace came. The Vlamertinghe road was remetalled; the village cleared of its grass-grown brickheaps, and old foundation sites marked out anew; the shell-holed fields were levelled by the shovels of Flemish, Poles, and Italians. A vast pile of "dud" shells and shell cases arose near "Goldfish" chateau.

The city of Ypres is clean and new and hybrid-English, its vast Grand Place holding enough air and sunlight to give a feeling of freedom and space.

The rectangular ruined fragment of the Cloth Hall is still contained in its scaffold box. Grass and wild flowers on the tops of the walls make the ruin beautiful. Jackdaws feed their young in the nests within the masonry gaps on high.

The less unobservant American visitors notice the four-way trumpets of the siren on the top of the ruin, and ask their guides if it is "the old original gas-horns of the British."

Alas, there is no historical thrill about that siren! It is a modern instrument, fixed there by the local fire brigade.

During the daytime the Grand Place is the parking-place for motor-cars and charabancs. A handbill may be put into your hand by a Belgian, an amusing document with its quaint spelling. "First-class cars for hire. Competition impossible." Well, there is nothing like downright statements for impressing the ignorant.

"Carefull (sic) drivers. Highly recommended and very popular with visitors' tours to Belgium, the prices quoted are for first-class car, including an experienced guide explaining all places of interest, visited or passed, and are inclusive, absolutely nothing extra."

You may go to Schrapnell (sic) corner, or Tyne cole (sic) cemetery ("absolutely largest in the district, about 12,000 graves"), or the "highly recommended and most interesting point of view, Trip No. 7," which includes "St. Julien, Poelcapelle, and the famous Houthulst forrest (sic), Deat (sic) trench, kept up in the state as it was during the war and can be visited for the small entrance fee of one franc."

DEATH TRENCH.

Death Trench, kept up in the same state as during the war, for three halfpence!

Don't you believe it, madam. You'll see nothing. If you could see it as it was (and it was an ideal home for a lounge-lizard compared with the Salient proper in '17) you would blench with pity and terror, and feel a hopeless misery when next you heard children in the front rows of cinemas booing the "cowardly villains" in a war film and cheering the "brave heroes." For the seeds of war are in every one of us; and only a broad, universal outlook can make war obsolete, like the burning of "witches."

Then there is Trip No. 9 . . . "after lunch a most extensive visit to Bruges (often referred to as the Venice of the North), including amongst others the Bloodchappel with the casket containing a drop of the Blood of Christ, brought back from Palestine by one of the Crusaders, with its famour paintings, recommended to all desiring a real pleasant and interesting day . . . £2 10s."

I know a woman, a parson's wife in a village in England, who went specially to see the Bloodchappel. The same woman solemnly declared to me, on an occasion when my remarks had affronted her ideals, that her best friend had "lost her husband in the war because she had loved him more than she had loved God," i.e., she had not gone to church on Sunday, but stayed at home or gone for walks with him.

Now let us seek a parallel in the annals of the highly-important, to wit, the "War Memories" of General von Ludendorff, where he writes of the battle of Tannenberg:—

> The enemy losses in killed and wounded, too, were extremely heavy. One of the most brilliant battles in the history of the world had been fought. To the training of our army in peace time alone did we owe this feat . . . (Then four paragraphs further on he says): In the Protestant church at Allenstein General von Hindenburg and I rendered thanks to Almighty God for this victory.

Both sincere patriots, this important general and the unimportant wife of a parson; both with minds of dead tissue (white sepulchres, to use another's metaphor).

Multiply this type of mind one hundred million times, with its every thought and action on the same level, and you get your wars between nations, each declaring its belief in its national righteousness under heaven.

TELEPHONE 322 **C. Rolander's Motor Car excursions from Ypres** 27, Rue de Dixmude YPRES

First class cars for hire | **Extremely moderate charges**
Competition impossible | **Experienced and carefull drivers**

The following motor trips from Ypres are highly recommended and very popular with visitors to Belgium, the prices quoted are **for a first class car to hold 6 passengers,** *including an experienced driver-guide explaining all places of interest, visited or passed, and are inclusive, absolutley nothing extra.*

£ - S - D

Trip. N° 1. — **Round about Ypres :** Visit to all places of interest in the town. Ruins of Cloth-Hall, Town hall, Cathedral, Irish fusilieres monument, ramparts, cemetery, Lille Gate, Menin Gate, Old Harbour, Ruins of the old pumping station, and return to Grand' Place . . . . 0 - 5 - 0

Trip. N° 2. — **Battle-field tour North of Ypres :** Leave from Ypres by the Dixmude-road and passing by White house cemetery, St. Jean, crossing the German first lines at Whiltchire, St. Julien, Canadian monument, Zonnebeke, St. Charles French cemetery, Sanctuary wood, Hill 62, Hellfire corner, Zillebeke, Hill 60, Railway dugouts, Schrapnell corner, and return to Ypres by Lille Gate . . . . . 0 - 12 - 6

Trip. N° 3. — **Extended battle-field tour North :** Leave Ypres the same way as in trip N° 2, continuing from St. Julien to Poelcappelle, visiting the monument of the famous French airman Guynemer brought down by the Germans near Poelcappelle, West-Roosebeke, Passchendaele ridge, Tyne cote cemetery, (largest in the district about 12.000 graves), Gheluvelt, Menin-road, Clapham Junction, Hooghe, Hill 62, Hellfire corner, Zillebeke, Hill 60, Railway dugouts, Schrapnell corner and return to Ypres by Lille Gate. . 1 - 0 - 0

Trip. N° 4. — **Battle-field tour South of Ypres :** Leave Ypres by Lille Gate, passing by Bedford House, St. Eloi, Wytschaete, with its famous minecrater, Kemmel, visiting the famous but from which is seen the most wonderfull panorama of the Salient, return to Ypres by La Clytte, Hallebast, Dickebusch, Kruisstraat, railway station, Grand' Place . . . . 0 - 12 - 6

Trip. N° 5. — **Extended Battle-field tour South** : Leave Ypres same way as trip. N° 4, proceding from Wytschaete to Messines, Ploegsteert, Armentiers, Nieppe, Le Seau, Neuve-Eglise, Lindehoek, Kemmel, Vierstraat, Kruisstraathoek and Lille Gate to Grand' Place, £ 1 - 0 - 0, plus cost of crossing French borders. This trip may be cut across from Ploegsteert by Romarin direct to Neuve-Eglise, which saves the expence incured going over the French border, entirely left to the choise of the customers.

Trip. N° 6. — **Lille :** A magnificent afternoon-drive of about 50 miles, passing by Menin, Halluin, Tourcoing and Roubaix, visits to the principal and most interesting parts of the Capital of the North of France . . 1 - 10 - 0
Plus fee for crossing the border.

Trip. N° 7. — **Dixmude :** A most interesting drive of about 45 miles, through the German and the British lines all the way. Passing by St. Julien, Poelcappelle and the famous Houthulst forrest, Houthulst, Clercken, Dixmude, visits to all interesting points as the Minottery, Deat-trench kept up in the same state as during the war and can be visited for the small entrance-fee of one franc, returning to Ypres by Woumen, Boesinghe making a short halt at the Irish farm cemetery and dressing Station. This is a very popular trip by visitors to Ypres and from interesting point of view Highly recommended . . . . 1 - 5 - 0

Trip. N° 8. — **Courtrai :** A charming afternoon drive of about 40 miles on the best road round about Ypres, to one of the biggest spinning centres in Belgium . . . . 1 - 5 - 0

ALL DAY TRIPS. -- Leave Ypres about 8.30 p. m.

Trip. N° 9. — **Bruges :** A most glorious drive of 80 miles, including the Battle-field and visit to the most interesting town in Belgium with its Canals and old building of 7 and 800 years of age. Leave from Ypres by Poelcappelle, Houthulst forrest, Clercken, Dixmude, Cockelaere, Leugenboom, where a halt is made, to visit the Big Canon (Lange Max) with which the Germans bombarded Dunkerque, and than proceding to Bruges via Ghistelles, passing trough a most beautifull Avenue, about 18 miles long and the best motoring road in Belgium. After lunch a most extensive visit of Bruges (often referred to as the Venice of the North) including amongst other the Bloodchappel with the cashet containing a drop of the Blood of Christ, brought back from Palestine by one of the Crusaders, the Townhall, with its famous paintings, the Gruit Huis, a trip on the old canals by motor boat, Memlings Museum, Cathedral, Beguinage, afternoon-tea and return to Ypres by Thourout, Hooglede, West-Roosebeke, St. Julien. This is a trip par exellence and Highly recommended to all desiring a real pleasant and interesting day . . . . 2 - 10 - 0

Trip. N° 10. — a) **Ostende :** Direct to catch boat to Dover . . . . 2 - 5 - 0
b) **Ostende :** Visit all day including Battle-field, Big Canon, Trenches at Nieuport, floaded area, etc. 2 - 15 - 0

Trip. N° 11. — **Bruxelles :** Visit to Place where Nurse Cavelle was shot, Avenue Louise and outer Boulevards, visit to unknown Soldiers Tomb, Royal Palace, Botanic gardens. A delightfull drive of about 150 miles, passing trough Gent and Alost . . . . 4 - 10 - 0

Trip. N° 12. — **Gent, St. Nicolas, Antwerp :** A charming drive right trough the two Flanders of about 170 miles, passing trough Menin, Courtrai, Gent, Lokeren, St. Nicolas, crossing the river Escaut by ferry (with the car), making a tour round Antwerp to visit principal and most interesting parts of the town and Docks, Zoological gardens, etc. A very nice drive on very good roads . . . . 5 - 0 - 0

Specialy reduced prices for bigger parties where two or more cars are required. — Special excursions to any part of Belgium, France or Holland, at very moderate cost, bussiness and private trips a specialty. — Visits to cemeteries and information in regards to wargraves, etc.

All bookings for this excursions are to be adressed to C. ROLANDER, 27, Rue de Dixmude, Telephone 322, YPRES (Café, Garage De Londres) and if possible before 6 p. m. day previous to leaving for excursions.

NB Henry's underlining of the word 'Schrapnell' – see *The Wet Flanders Plain.*

—AND THIS WAS YPRES.—III.

HOW TROOP TRAINS ARRIVED AT "POP."

HOTEL SKINDLES.

By HENRY WILLIAMSON.

(This is the third of a series of articles by an ex-soldier describing a tour of the battlefields.)

THE troop trains arriving at Poperinghe by day used to behave peculiarly as they approached the station. Card parties squatting on the wooden floors of the trucks were liable to be thrown forwards, jerked upright, and flung backwards.

Cling! clang! plonk! plink! crank! ran from buffer to buffer along the grey length of the train. Then another jerk, the frantic puffing of an engine whose wheels were racing on the rails, and the train went on, faster and faster, rattling through the station, and stopping half a mile past it.

Then perhaps we might hear a noise filling the air as though the sky were a dome of solid glass, and an immense diamond were cutting a slow curve down it—a hard noise, as of gem-hard dust being ground away.

As it drew nearer it changed to a coarse vibration of steel, opening a furrow in the very heavens, droning, buzzing, hissing, dropping in scale to a deep bass and growing louder and louder, a noise enormous and terrifying; and then a geyser of black smoke and wooden sleepers and stones arose, a rending metallic cra-ash, a great deep smoking crater under rails twisted and blue-scaled with heat, the whining "zip" of hot splinters, and the thudding down of lumps of wood and earth. A seventeen-inch howitzer shell, fired from a dozen miles away, from behind one of those ridges the taking of which cost nearly half a million casualties in 1917.

* * *

We walked out of Poperinghe station, making our way to the Rue d'Hôpital, to find Talbot House, the "Toc H" of history. It was identified by its position next to the chemist's shop, by its greyish-white painted front three storeys high, and iron outer gates.

I called in at the chemist's shop to ask if it would be possible to see the chapel in the hop-loft, where many thousands of men had received the Blessed Sacrament before going up to the Passchendaele battles. The chemist did not remember me, of course; but I recollected that face, slightly like the photographs of Hindenburg. (He was very angry when in 1917 I remarked the likeness during the purchase of plaster for blistered feet.)

The chemist said that the owner of "Toc H" would welcome our visit. I said, "Thank you, monsieur. Do you remember my telling you ten years ago that you were like a famous—pardon, a notorious enemy general?"

I could see that his ideas had not changed.

* * *

We rang the bell of the tall grey house. Almost at once the inner door opened, and a young girl appeared. She opened the gates, and drew back with a movement quiet and charming, bidding us enter. Our nailed shoes clattered on the tiled floor.

"To see the chapel, messieurs?" She led the way up the bare, white-enamelled stairs, into a room austerely furnished, up another flight, and then to a door, which she held open for us before leaving with a slight movement of her head, neither bow nor nod, but a gesture of sensibility and understanding.

Up the last flight, very steep, of poplar wood, unpainted and thin—worn by 40,000 nailed boots clumping up and clumping down. We sat on the bench at the far end, where the altar—an old carpenter's bench—used to stand. Silence filled the wooden hollow of the loft, with its whitewashed rafters stained brown where rain had dripped through tiles, and its smooth bare floorboards showing the holes gouged by the goat-moth caterpillar in the living trees.

Twenty thousand souls, bearing names bestowed upon them with pride and tenderness by twenty thousand mothers, clumping up the steep and narrow way, borne there by Hope, and seeking solace at the very verge of Darkness!

The sun came out of a cloud, and light shone whiter through the five semi-circular windows. Sparrows could be heard chirping on the roof, and the slow rattle of wheels on the pavé of the road below. Far away there was a dull report. They were blowing up the artillery concrete "pillboxes" in the fields near Brandhoek.

After our rest and silent communion we clumped down the narrow stairs for the second, and maybe the last, time, and went on our way, bearing a fresh layer in memory, of youthful charm, grave and impersonal, waiting on two unknown English pilgrims.

* * *

In June 1916 an officer in the Rifle Brigade, enjoying eggs and chips and a bottle of wine in a certain estaminet in "Pop," declared to his friends that it was as good a pub, as Skindles at Maidenhead. The estaminet had already a longish name painted on its front—Hotel de la Bourse du Houblon something or other—but no one took any notice of that.

The British officers began to call it Skindles, and very soon the three rooms on the ground floor were crowded with tables, and the tables with bottles; and around the bottles (for the water of the country was condemned for drinking purposes) sat the British officers, smoking, laughing, eating, or wanting to eat, and shouting the name of Zoe, which was the name of the daughter of the "Mother of the Soldiers," as madame was called.

The officer of the Rifle Brigade was killed on the Somme a few weeks later, as were many of his friends; and now, eleven years after, his memory is still fresh in the minds of Zoë and the "Mother of the Soldiers." The "original" Skindles in "Pop" has returned to its former easy comfort and prices.

* * *

The Hotel Skindles, we thought, might possibly be too expensive for our meagre wad of notes, and so we clumped along the Rue d'Hôpital until we found what looked like a cheap place. We were met by a young and comely woman with a reserved and pleasant smile on her countenance. We asked for an omelette. Toute de suite!

Chairs were piled on the long table inside, on which lay a soiled and worn American cloth.

We waited half an hour. The room was dreary and lifeless. Should we walk out? It looked, perhaps, too cheap a place. But no; we might disappoint the young woman with the Mona Lisa smile.

We waited. A smell of burning stole into the room. Still, it might be only the egg-shells. Then came the young woman, with the same fixed and pleasant expression, bearing a yellow and black omelette. She put it before us, with slices of bread. We asked for butter. Butter? Yes, butter. Toute de suite.

We scraped off the unburned part of the omelette, washing it down with a bottle of ordinary cheap white wine. Ah, well, it didn't pay always to be too economical.

Outside, we looked at the name of the place. "To Trustfulness." We laughed, and for some kilometres along the road to Ypres were withering the patron, or his detachable wraith accompanying us, with ironical speeches.

THE MENIN GATE PRAYER.

The following prayer, drawn up by the Archbishop of Canterbury, will be used on Sunday, at the opening of the Menin Gate Memorial to the 55,000 British soldiers who lost their lives at the Ypres Salient, and who have no known graves:—

ALMIGHTY and most merciful Father, God of the spirits of all flesh, Who by Thy Blessed Son has taught us to know the wishes of Thy Love, we remember before Thee, to Whom the unknown are yet well known, the great company of our brothers who laid down their lives for their country, but whose earthly resting place no man knoweth.

In thankfulness and hope we commend their souls to Thy gracious keeping, and we beseech Thee to grant that, as we raise their memorial, so we may walk worthy of their fellowship, through Him Who was dead and is alive, our Lord and Saviour Jesus Christ. Amen.

CANCELLED SHOW LOSS.

£3,000 ESTIMATE NOT COVERED BY INSURANCE.

"Daily Express" Correspondent.

TUNBRIDGE WELLS, Thursday.

The loss caused by the cancellation of the Tunbridge Wells and South-Eastern Counties Agricultural Show—which was not insured—may be £3,000, according to Sir George Courthope, chairman of the council, who said today that it was too soon to go into the figures.

Many horses left by permission overnight, and the poultry and rabbit section is practically cleared. It is expected that the cattle, sheep, pigs, and goats will remain isolated for a few days pending further orders from the Ministry of Agriculture.

BE

HOTEL SKINDLES
- YPRES -
Phone : YPRES 3
En face de la Gare
- Opposite Station -
Telegr. :
SKINDLES Ypres
Sous le Haut Patronage de S. A. R. la Princesse BEATRICE (Angl.)
Under the distinguished patron. of H. R. H. the Princess BEATRICE (Engl.)
Most modern and up to date
Hotel in the salient
Home comforts. Reading Room
Baths-Hot and Gold
Excellent cuisine
English speaking staff
The Original SKINDLES at
POPERINGHE
43, Hospitalstreet
Conforts modernes
Cuisine des plus renommées
de la Flandre
Salon de lecture au 1er étage
Même Établissement
POPERINGHE
43, Rue de l'Hôpital

From a postcard in Henry Williamson's archive

I BELIEVE IN

THE MEN WHO DIED

BY HENRY WILLIAMSON.

This most moving and brilliantly written article, by the winner of the Hawthornden Prize for 1928, is in continuance of the now famous " Daily Express" new series in which distinguished men and women are reaffirming their faith in certain things that, to them, matter most in life. Among forthcoming contributors will be Viscount Castlerosse, Editor of the much-discussed "Londoner's Log" in the "Sunday Express"; May Edginton, author of many short stories, novels, and films; Hannen Swaffer, Humbert Wolfe, and Ethel Mannin, the novelist.

THE church in the peaceful village where I live has a tower of grey stone, in which is a belfry. A clock with gilt hands and Roman numerals shines in the southern wall. It was built into the tower as a memorial to those men of the parish who fell in the great war. Down in the porch is an illuminated scroll with a list of the names of those who made the great sacrifice.

Sometimes, when the ringers go up into the room where hang the ropes with the coloured sallies, I go with them, climbing on up the worn stone steps of the dim spiral stairway, to the bells. The ropes and wheels begin to creak; the bells begin to swing, and the tower trembles. Then with a dinning crash the metal tongues smite the deep bronze mouths, and an immense torrent of sound pours out of the narrow doorway.

* * *

and my limbs tremble and stiffen as in an icicle while the gaping, smoking parapet above the rim of my helmet spurts and lashes with machine-gun bullets. . . .

Until in the flame and the rolling smoke I see men arising and walking forward; and I go forward with them, as in a nightmare wherein some seem to pause, with bowed heads, and sink carefully to their knees, and roll slowly over, and lie still. Others roll and roll, and scream and grip my legs in uttermost fear, and I have to struggle to break away, while the dust and earth on my tunic changes from grey to red . . . .

And I go on with aching feet, up and down over ground like a huge ruined honeycomb, and my

SCHOOLBOYS OF TO-DAY.

our guns are "back on the first objective," and Kitchener's Army, with all its hopes and beliefs, has found its grave on those northern slopes of the Somme battlefield.

A year drifts by, and I am standing on a duckboard by a flooded and foul beek in the salient, listening in the flare-pallid rainy darkness to the cries of tens of thousands of wounded men lost in the morasses of third Ypres. To seek them is to drown with them. . . . The living are still toiling on, homeless and without horizons, doing dreadful things under heaven that none want to do, through the long wet days and the longer nights, the weeks, the months, of a bare sodden winter out of doors.

The survivors are worn out; some of them, tested beyond

war, my dear chap; it's deep in human nature." They may say, as a friendly tip, "Don't talk about the war before my young son, old man, if you don't mind. He's going into the Navy, and I don't want him unsettled. You know what youngsters are—very impressionable."

Sometimes things seem even more hopeless, as when I hear a few hundred school children, marched to the local picture palace for patriotic purposes, cheering and yelling at a film, which only faintly suggests reality, called "The Somme," frantically cheering the "British heroes," and booing the "German cowards," even when one poor lad in grey, who went forth to fetch water for a dying comrade, was knocked over by a shell.

The children, I know, are but distorting mirrors of a grown-up mental attitude; but surely, after all these nineteen centuries, it is time that people should begin to know what they do.

Last year, nearly ten years after the war, I was called a traitor by [illegible]

The great sound sweeps other thought away into the air, and the earth fades; the powerful wraith of those four years of the war enters into me, and the torrent becomes the light and clangour of massed guns that thrall the senses.

I take the weight and strength of the barrage, and grow mighty with it, until it becomes but a seam of sound nicked with flashes and puny in space and time controlled by the vaster roar of stars in their age-long travail through elemental darkness. I see all life created by those flaming suns of the night, and out of life arises a radiance, wan and phantasmal and pure, the light of Khristos.

The wraith of the war, glimmering with this inner vision, bears me to the wide and shattered country of the Somme, to every broken wood and trench and sunken lane, among the broad straggling belts of rusty wire smashed and twisted in the chalky loam, while the ruddy clouds of brick-dust hang over the shelled villages by day, and at night the eastern horizon roars and bubbles with light.

And everywhere in these desolate places I see the faces and figures of enslaved men, the marching columns pearl-hued with chalky dust on the sweat of their heavy drab clothes; the files of carrying parties laden and staggering in the flickering moonlight of gun-fire; the "waves" of assaulting troops lying silent and pale on the tape-lines of the jumping-off places . . . .

Again I crouch with them while the steel glacier rushing by just overhead scrapes away every syllable, every fragment of a message bawled into my ear, while my mind begins to stare fixedly into the bitter dark of imminent death,

". . . . Here I see plainly how the hope of the world lies in the child. We must free the child . ."
—Henry Williamson, in the accompanying article.

wave melts away, and the second wave comes up, and also melts away, and then the third wave merges into the ruins of the first and second, and after a while the fourth blunders into the remnants of the others, and we begin to run forward to catch up with the barrage, gasping and sweating, in bunches, anyhow, every bit of the months of drill and rehearsal forgotten, for who could have imagined that the big push was going to be like this?

We come to wire that is uncut, and beyond we see grey coal-scuttle helmets bobbing about, and the steam of over-heated machine-guns wafting away in the fountainous black smoke of howitzer shells; and the loud crackling of the machine-guns changes to a screeching as of steam being blown off by a hundred engines; and soon no one is left standing. And an hour later breaking point, put the muzzle of their rifles in their mouths, in the darkness of the terrible nights, and pull the trigger. Those at home, sitting in armchairs and talking proudly of patriotism and heroism, will never realise the bitter contempt and scorn the soldiers have for those and other abstractions; the soldiers feel they have been betrayed by the high-sounding phrases that heralded the war, for they know that the enemy soldiers are the same men as themselves, suffering and disillusioned in exactly the same way. . . . .

* * *

I leave my bells and descend to earth again; and if I try to explain why I want to re-live those old days, to tear the truth out of the past, perhaps some one will say to me, "Oh, the war! A tragedy, wasn't it? It is best forgotten," or, "There always will be

a certain old man because I dared to suggest that our duty to our fellow men should not end at the cliffs of Dover; so I returned to my old comrades in the scarred and rolling country of the Somme and the Hindenburg Line.

* * *

Here, in the beautiful desolation of rush and willow in the tracts unploughed, the narrow and selfish ideals of nationalism are not set hard; men do not despise and hate others they have never seen. Here I see plainly how the hope of the world lies in the child. We must free the child, let its mind grow itself like green corn, and all will be well. Putting on the abstract virtues of form, tradition, reverence, to an ungrown mind is to produce something unnatural, false, and death-bringing.

The faceless corruption of Ypres was the grave of the old-world ideals! The virtues must develop from within, from the imagination, not from any forms of idolatry. The summer is beautiful to men of all nations, and every man was once a little boy with an imagination.

I have a little boy now; a wild little innocent who looks at birds in the sky, at poppies and bumble-bees and dandelions, and thinks no mean thought, and sees no harm anywhere. His little friends in the village play at trains and "moti-cars" with him; he calls me "Daddy Wee," and runs away to be chased with cries of delight. Must he, too, with those friends, traverse a waste place of the earth; must the blood and sweat of his generation drip in agony, where poppies have grown, and corn?

2

(Apologia)

as a friendly hint, 'Don't talk about the war before my
boy, old chap, if you don't mind. I don't want him
unsettled: you know what youngsters are — very impressionable.
And after all, there is such a thing as loyalty to one's
country, you know."

2

Sometimes it seems even more hopeless, as when I
saw a few hundred school children, marched to the local picture
palace for patriotic purposes, cheering ~~spasmodically~~ & booing at a film
which only faintly suggests reality, called 'The Somme', ~~frantically~~
frantically cheering ~~the poor lads in~~ the ~~(apparently unfatigued~~
"British heroes" in their ~~[illegible]~~ immaculate uniforms, and booing
the "German cowards" who chaps seemed to be hurrying away
from the heroic onrush (shades of the 8th Division at
Thiepval!). They booed even when one poor lad in grey,
who went forth to fetch water for a dying comrade,
was knocked over by a shell.

The children, I know, are but the distorting mirrors of a
grown-up mental attitude; but surely, after the bitter ~~[illegible]~~
agony, waste of the lost generation of Europe, it is time that
people should begin to know what they do.

This year, nearly ten years after the war, I was called a traitor by my father
(once I was his little boy) because I dared to suggest that ~~[illegible]~~ honour and duty
~~a certain old man~~ ~~to humanity~~ I ~~our fellow men~~ become our fellow men stood not end at the Straits of ~~Dover, so~~ Dover. It was a
sad scene; more poignant than ~~the [illegible] Passchendaele~~, the Hindenburg Line. ~~So~~ I could ~~lose~~ ~~mind~~ remain there; it was agony ~~[illegible]~~; so I

I returned to my old comrades in the scarred and rolling
country of the Somme, ~~at the Hindenburg Line, to meet them in~~ live with me
~~spirit~~, for I am dead with them, and they have quickened out of
again. ~~To~~ There I ~~learned~~ renewed the truths which ~~the Somme was the grave of the~~
deaths: ~~that the corruption~~ (the truth) of ~~Ypres & the Somme~~ ~~is important to all men that inspired~~ ~~[illegible]~~
~~old world~~: ~~that the chief [illegible] freed from the ideals that inspired~~ that human values are superior to those of national gun; the universal, making all life one, but that
~~generated the savagery~~ ~~[illegible]~~ arise ~~by~~ the laughter of the spirit; that ~~[illegible]~~ ~~in its own~~; that we must free the
idolatry, which do not ~~[illegible]~~ multiply while men are brothers, and the laughter of ~~[illegible]~~
~~universal, and the~~ laughter;
child from all things that maintain the ideals of a narrow nationalism, the ideals which inspired ~~[illegible]~~ generated the barrages in which ~~their laughter~~ ten million men ~~[illegible]~~ ~~[illegible]~~, their laughter ~~[illegible]~~ ~~ten million men~~ ~~laughing, willing~~ were ~~[illegible]~~ completed, perished.

I BELIEVE IN THE MEN WHO DIED

BY HENRY WILLIAMSON, Hawthornden Prize Winner for 1928. Author of "The Pathway."

We have received numerous requests from our readers to reprint this article by an ex-officer in the British Army which appeared in the "Daily Express" of 17th September, 1928. We are able to comply with their wishes by the kind permission of Mr. Henry Williamson and by the courtesy of the Editor of the "Daily Express."

The church in the peaceful village where I live has a tower of grey stone, in which is a belfry. A clock with gilt hands and Roman numerals shines in the southern wall. It was built into the tower as a memorial to those men of the parish who fell in the great war. Down in the porch is an illuminated scroll with a list of the names of those who did not come home.

Sometimes, when the ringers go up into the room where hang the ropes with the coloured sallies, I go with them, climbing on up the worn stone steps of the dim spiral stairway, to the bells. The ropes and wheels begin to creak; the bells begin to swing, and the tower trembles. Then with a dinning crash the metal tongues smite the deep bronze mouths, and an immense torrent of sound pours out of the narrow doorway.

The great sound sweeps other thought away into the air, and the earth fades; the powerful wraith of those four years of the war enters into me, and the torrent becomes the light and clangour of massed guns that thrall the senses.

I take the weight and strength of the barrage, and grow mighty with it, until it becomes but a seam of sound nicked with flashes and puny in space and time controlled by the vaster roar of stars in their age-long travail through elemental darkness. I see all life created by those flaming suns of the night, and out of life arises a radiance, wan and phantasmal and pure, the light of Khristos.

The wraith of the war, glimmering with this inner vision, bears me to the wide and shattered country of the Somme, to every broken wood and trench and sunken lane, among the broad, straggling belts of rusty wire, smashed and twisted in the chalky loam, while the ruddy clouds of brickdust hang over the shelled villages by day, and at night the eastern horizon roars and bubbles with light.

And everywhere in these desolate places I see the faces and figures of enslaved men, the marching columns pearl-hued with chalky dust on the sweat of their heavy drab clothes; the files of carrying parties laden and staggering in the flickering moonlight of gunfire; the "waves" of assaulting troops lying silent and pale on the tape-lines of the jumping-off places.

Again I crouch with them while the steel glacier rushing by just overhead scrapes away every syllable, every fragment of a message bawled into my ear, while my mind begins to stare fixedly into the bitter dark of imminent death, and my limbs tremble and stiffen as in an icicle, while the gaping, smoking parapet above the rim of my helmet spurts and lashes with machine-gun bullets.

Until in the flame and the rolling smoke I see men arising and walking forward; and I go forward with them, as in a nightmare wherein some seem to pause, with bowed heads, and sink carefully to their knees, and roll slowly over, and lie still. Others roll and roll, and scream and grip my legs in uttermost fear, and I have to struggle to break away, while the dust and earth on my tunic changes from grey to red.

And I go on with aching feet, up and down over ground like a huge ruined honeycomb, and my wave melts away, and the second wave comes up, and also melts away, and then the third wave merges into the ruins of the first and second, and after a while the fourth blunders into the remnants of the others, and we begin to run forward to catch up with the barrage, gasping and sweating, in bunches, anyhow, every bit of the months of drill and rehearsal forgotten, for who could have imagined that the big push was going to be like this?

We come to wire that is uncut, and beyond we see grey coal-scuttle helmets bobbing about, and the steam of over-heated machine-guns wafting away in the fountainous black smoke of howitzer shells; and the loud crackling of the machine-guns changes to a screeching as of steam being blown off by a hundred engines; and soon no one is left standing. And an hour later our guns are "back on the first objective," and Kitchener's Army, with all its hopes and beliefs, has found its grave on those northern slopes of the Somme battlefield.

A year drifts by, and I am standing on a duckboard by a flooded and foul beck in the Salient, listening in the flare-pallid rainy darkness to the cries of tens of thousands of wounded men lost in the morasses of third Ypres. To seek them is to drown with them . . . The living are still toiling on, homeless and without horizons, doing dreadful things under heaven that none want to do, through the long wet days and the longer nights, the weeks, the months, of a bare, sodden winter out of doors.

The survivors are worn out; some of them, tested beyond breaking point, put the muzzles of their rifles in their mouths, in the darkness of the terrible nights and pull the trigger.

Those at home, sitting in armchairs and talking proudly of patriotism and heroism, will never realise the bitter contempt and scorn the soldiers have for these and other abstractions; the soldiers feel they have been betrayed by the high-sounding phrases that heralded the war, for they know that the enemy soldiers are the same men as themselves, suffering and disillusioned in exactly the same way.

And in the stupendous roar and light-blast of the final barrage that broke the Hindenburg line I see only one thing, which grows radiant before my eyes until it fills all my world: the sight of a Saxon boy half crushed under a shattered tank, moaning "Mutter, mutter, mutter," out of ghastly grey lips. A British soldier, wounded in the leg, and sitting nearby, hears the words, and, dragging himself to the dying boy, takes his cold hand and says: "All right, son, it's all right. Mother's here with you."

The bells cease and I descend again to the world of the living, and move among men who did not go through the fire, and who think the old thoughts, and who seem not to care that it will happen again unless all believe in the

The Last Hundred Days of the War

August 8,1918.

Says Ludendorff,"August 8th was the black day of the German Army in the history of this war.This was the worst experience I had to go through."

The night of the 7th--8th,in the Somme country between the Ancre and the Somme--a broken wilderness fought over three times before--was damp and very quiet;and three hours after midnight a dense white mist began to drift up the river valley.So thick was it that the infantry and tanks waiting at their jumping-off points--(white tape-lines had been laid-out in places a few hours previously)-prepared to move entirely by prismatic compass.Voices came ghostly muffled and from a yard ahead;" khaki uniforms were silvered by the mist,like air-bubbles in human shapes grotesque moving under s strange grey sea.

Here and there along the 20-mile front small knots of staff officers waited anxiously.Some days before a German raid had captured a Australian sergeant and some men;and if in the cross examination the enemy had been given any cause for suspicion,their guns would open before zero,and smash the waiting assault.

Four o'clock.All silent.The chill vapour eddied and swirled; settled thick again.The British 4th Army,consisting of 14 divisions of English,Canadian,Australian,and American divisions,with a cavalry corps,had moved only at night,hiding by day; after empty train empty train had gone north, observed by enemy observation balloons;the guns massed had not registered.Success depened on complete surprise The 1st French Army was to operate between Montidier and Rpye,another 12 divisions.Had these hundreds of tho sands of men,and their immense ~~mass~~ encumbrance of war material--scores of miles of transport lorries, waggons,guns,etc--been entirely unsuspected?

4.15 hours.Silence.The Germans were dug-in among half-ruined cornfields,many miles from their dreadful steel-and -concrete Siegfried Stellung(Hindenburg Line) which they had left in the great drive of March 21.

4.16 hours. British and Colonial officers,unifiemed exactly like their men,stare fixedy at their wristlet watches.Four minutes to go!Still silence,clammy cold grey mist."Uneartly silence", thought many.

4.20.The mist flickers;becomes soaked with light;burdened with the steel glaciers of shells which scrape away every other sound from the ear.The bubbling brightness is overcome by the earth on fire,and men moving slowly behind walls of smoke and spouting flame.They move on,and on,leaving few dead and wounded.The mist grows thinner,and vanished in sunshine;and miles behind the enemy front lines tanks are lurching,surprising division and corps headquarters staffs at breakfast,and leaving their terrible visiting cards through walls,doors, and windows.

At last a real "Gap",longed for by the cavalry during four slow,dreary years:but where is the old Kitchener's Army that dreamed of these things? For two years the wreckage of its hope has lain on tis very Somme battlefield.The War has lasted too long.

Well,people in England were much cheered.Last night the Premier annonced in the Commons the destruction of 150 U Boats;and tonight,August 8,1918,they read of the break-through,with 13,000 prisoners and 200 guns taken by the 4th Army(rawlinson's).

The Last Hundred Days of the War

10 August 1918.

The battle of Amiens is slowing up;many of the tanks working with English,Canadian,and Australian troops are shattered and burnt out;the infantry is tired,and ~~heavy with want of sleep~~. ~~The enemy~~ has been blowing up his ammunition dumps all the previous night;~~and is~~ back ~~at~~ the old trench systems he held at the beginning of the battle of the Somme in 1916.

However,~~we~~ go forward again today.~~With the Canadians,owing~~ to ~~the~~ orders being issued late,the hour of attack has been altered,and it ~~took~~ place in broad daylight without smoke screens.The tanks suffer,twenty three out of forty three receiving direct hits.~~The~~ grass-grown trench systems of ~~1916~~,with their maze of trenches and subsided dugouts ~~prevented any~~ chance of a rapid advance in the face of the cross-fire the sweeping ~~of machine guns~~.

The Tank Corps reserves ~~were~~ are used up;~~and~~ the ~~machines~~ and their crews fought almost to a standstill.After an average of three hours in aclosed tank, in action,all men began to suffer from severe headaches and giddiness,and most from sickness,a high temperature and heart disturbance(The popular films ten years later did show the realities of action:that is why those who ~~went through it~~ sat ed quiet and still and ~~slightly~~ hopeless while the young cheer and ~~laugh)~~.

Today there have been many"dog-fights" in the air.48 enemy machines have been destroyed,and 17 driven down out of control. 50 British 'planes failed to come home~~;and the nights in the~~ squadron messes ~~were~~ more hectic than usual...for tomorrow...

The German Great General Main Headquarters ~~was~~ very disturbed.

(3)

The Last Hundred Days.

by

Henry Williamson

18 August, ~~1928~~. 1918.

This morning, being a Sunday, our troops attacked

up north, in the Ypres district.

~~Yesterday, a Saturday,~~

Owing to the difficulty of bringing up guns over the half-broken

gained ~~with many war-sick prisoners~~

country ~~left by the~~ ~~[illegible]~~ from the ~~Germans~~ during the

the enemy, ~~with many war-sick prisoners~~, into the old

during past week, the attack planned for 13th August

Somme country was cancelled. ~~The 4th Army~~

guns & ammunition

Owing to the immense difficulty of bringing up

gained from the enemy during

over the half-broken country proposed last Sunday morning

the past week, the ~~further~~ attack by the 4th Army ~~was~~

cancelled, much to the relief of new drafts to the infantry — both British & German — who had ~~were~~ were now made

been "for it." Many of the ~~battalions~~ ~~are~~ ~~composed now of~~ young boys

young boys, ~~unable~~ who while most ~~thought~~ ~~[illegible]~~ with so much of their fortified themselves before coming out, against the idea of death,

up almost entirely of

the ruthlessness ~~of~~ & involvement of war

Nomans in England: and [Today, Sunday, a scorching hot day, they read in what are usually called the 'Comic Cuts' — ~~the~~ Corps ~~Summaries~~ Summaries as the Corps give way to despair.

make many

'Comic Cuts', — During the last nine days, since the opening of the ~~present~~ most

successful ~~[illegible]~~, in the war, the 4th Army. has ~~defeated~~ pushed the British back to a depth of 12 miles; has

drove the enemy no less than 27 of the

engaged with its own 13 divisions prisoners and ~~4000~~ 400

enemy's; has taken over ~~[illegible]~~ 20,000 ~~killed~~ ~~wounded~~ ~~wounded~~

guns. ~~& killed~~ the 4th Army suffered 27,000

(Ten years later history shows that about the same number of

casualties, while killing outright the enemy. The colossal blast of ~~tank~~ ~~the~~ the 2000-gun barrage, the

surprise of the vast ~~tank~~ secret concentration of & of troops & tanks, & the comparative

Henry

For H. Williamson

DURRANT'S PRESS CUTTINGS,

St. Andrew's House, 32 to 34 Holborn Viaduct,
and 3 St. Andrew Street, Holborn Circus, E.C.1.
Telephone: CITY 4963.

Daily Express
8 Shoe Lane, E.C.4.

Cutting from issue dated 11 AUG 1928 192

The Last 100 Days.

By HENRY WILLIAMSON.
Winner of the Hawthornden Prize for 1928.

Ten years ago this week there began at Amiens the series of terrific engagements that were to culminate in the final collapse of the German military machine. The "Daily Express" has asked Mr. Henry Williamson, who served as a soldier of the line, to describe from time to time in these columns the principal events of the last hundred days of the war.

August 11, 1918.

The great battle of Amiens is slowing up. Many of the tanks working with the English and Colonial troops are shattered and burned out. The infantry is tired, and lying out in the flattened cornfields alongside the numerous German dead. "Jerry" has been blowing up his ammunition dumps during the previous night, before retiring to the trench systems he held at the beginning of the Somme battle in 1916. However, our tired men go forward again to-day. Owing to orders being issued late, the hour of the Canadian attack has been altered, and the assault takes place in broad daylight, without smoke screens from airplanes. The tanks suffer, twenty-three out of forty-three receiving direct hits from enemy field guns firing over open sights.

The remainder, stiflingly hot with petrol fumes, so that the crews have to breathe through the mouthpieces of their box-respirators, churn their way through the grass-grown hummocks and hollows of old trenches and subsided dug-outs, among rusty wire tangles, and willows springing out of old shell holes.

The reserves are exhausted; tanks and their crews have fought to a standstill. After an average three hours in a tank in action men begin to suffer from severe headaches and giddiness, sickness, and heart palpitation.

* * *

To-night in the squadron messes life is more hectic than usual; drink and be merry, for to-morrow . . . 48 enemy machines have been destroyed, 17 driven down out of control. Fifty British airplanes are missing.

At the enemy Main General Headquarters to-night it is reported to Ludendorff that the reserve German troops hurrying up by train and lorry are being greeted with cries of "Blackleg!" by the German soldiers trickling away from the battlefield.

Meanwhile the haggard, bloodshot-eyed, lethargic British and Dominion troops are relieved; in long, dogged strings they slouch away from the line, thinking only of sleep, sleep, sleep; slouching on, anywhere, anyhow, bent under rifles and equipment, puttees down over boots, feet swelled and shapeless, tottering with fatigue. . . .

The Last Hundred Days.

With The 4th Army.

By HENRY WILLIAMSON.
Winner of this year's Hawthornden Prize.

August 18, 1918.

Owing to the immense difficulty of bringing up guns and ammunition over the half-broken country gained from the enemy during the past week, the proposed attack by the 4th Army on Thursday morning was cancelled, much to the relief of those who had thought themselves "for it."

Many of the new drafts to the infantry—both British and German—are made up almost entirely of young boys, who think too much of their homes; and while most have fortified themselves, before coming out, against the idea of death, the ruthlessness and enslavement of war make many give way to despair.

To-day it is scorching hot on the old Somme battlefields, where they lie out in shallow trenches that are cut through the two-year-old wreckage of 1916. The platoon officers read in "Comic Cuts"—as the corps summaries are invariably called—that during the last nine days, since the opening of the most successful British push so far, the 4th Army has driven the enemy back to a depth of 12 miles; has engaged with its own 13 divisions no fewer than 27 of the enemy's; and has taken over 20,000 prisoners and 400 guns.

* * *

The colossal blasting power of the 2,000-gun barrage, the surprise of the vast secret concentration of troops and tanks, the comparatively unfortified enemy positions, and the war-weariness of the Germans accounted for this reversal of the usual casualty ratio—for until the last hundred days it was the French and British who lost two men for every one German.

This afternoon the news came over the field telephones and "buzzers" that a small attack by troops of the 3rd Army south of Bailleul was entirely successful. The village of Outtersteene and several fortified farms—their cellars made into pill-boxes of ferro-concrete with roofs a yard thick, and splayed with slits in the walls for machine-guns to fire through—near the railway line have been taken.

The enemy lines were pierced to a depth of 1,000-2,000 yards on a four-mile front. Merville, one of the towns taken in the big enemy drive in the spring, is expected to be evacuated during the night.

The remnants of one of the battalions coming out of this "small" action were given an issue of lime-juice instead of rum. The remarks of the "footsloggers" do not appear in any of the war histories, although it was officially stated that "the spirit of the troops is excellent."

4th article.

The Last Hundred Days.

(1)

21 August, 1918.

Today the 3rd Army has planned to launch an attack to the north of the Ancre with the object of getting within striking distance of the main enemy defensive position which is to be assaulted in two days time.

From eight o'clock onwards the previous night until 2 a.m. this morning, the infantry had been assembling on the tape-lines, the tanks waiting at their jumping-off points, the gunners working out the "lifts" of the barrage, the airplanes testing engines and machine guns for the attack on the enemy position along the heights above the Albert-Arras railway. Above the chill white ground mist bubbled and roared until the sky.

At 4.55 hours the infantry rose up & moved slowly forward at the arranged rate of 100 yards every 3 minutes, and the tanks began to churn their way forward into the enemy counter-barrage and hissing criss-cross of fire of hundreds of machine guns. The mist hid everything, no sight outside three or four yards, until nearly 11 hours (i.e. 11 a.m).

The front line was taken so easily that it was realized the enemy reserves were being kept for counter-attacks behind a lightly-held outpost line. The guns were scanty, too, obviously they had been withdrawn

Very suddenly, at 11 hours, the mist thinned & vanished, revealing to our men the Arras–Albert railway line. It proved to have been prepared as the enemy's main defence, being commanded at point-blank range by many field-guns; & all places where tanks could cross – where the line lay level, neither embanked nor laid in a cutting in the chalk — were not only

carefully registered, but were blocked ~~[illegible]~~ by ~~[illegible]~~

~~[illegible]~~ anti-tank stockades ~~[illegible]~~ of the well-known

set close together

Hindenburg-line pattern — lengths of rail ~~[illegible]~~

& rising diagonally out of huge concrete blocks.

at once

~~Immediately~~ whirlwinds of fire & earth circled about the

tanks, & within a few minutes thirty seven tanks were ~~[illegible]~~

smashed & ~~[illegible]~~ in flames. ~~[illegible]~~ But if the German

gunners could at last see the tanks, the British planes could

see the gunners, & dive at them with bomb & machine-gun fire.

[The fight ~~continued~~ lasted until the afternoon, when

many of the tanks' crews became unconscious and memory-losing

in the great heat; ~~[illegible]~~ and in others the ammunition swelled the hands, &

steering wheels ~~[illegible]~~ burned ~~[illegible]~~

& jamming the guns, smoking & blinding

were untouchable, ~~[illegible]~~

By nightfall the line of the railway was gained ~~[illegible]~~

almost entirely, with several villages & 2000 prisoners; and

~~on 25th were being~~ ~~[illegible]~~

~~preparations for the main attack of~~ tracks were thick

~~hastened.~~ all roads & men and mules & engines for the

~~[illegible]~~ with ~~preparation~~

main assault in two days time.

5th article.

The Last Hundred Days.

23 August 1918.

This morning at 4.45 hours the ghastly light of the moon above a thin mist on the stricken fields was flooded with the false flickering sunrise of a barrage, and along a thirty three mile front — from our junction with the French near the place near Mercatel where the Hindenburg line from Quéant & Bullecourt joined the old Arras–Vimy defence of 1916 — the assault opened with a hundred tanks, and men of the 3rd, 4th, 5th, and 6th Corps.

The German machine gunners defended their posts with extraordinary heroism — they were always brave troops — often firing their guns until the very moment when they & their weapons were crushed to the earth by the attacking tank. Every third cartridge in the belts feeding their guns held a copper-sheathed steel-cored bullet, and the tanks were pitted all over and in many places penetrated by these. As usual, many of the crews became delirious in the terrific heat inside the tanks, & some even the dreaded tanks with phosphorus bombs, filled them with smoke like cotton wool.

Messages dropped by aeroplanes were invaluable in keeping the whole straggling action in hand, & by giving the staff information. ~~For most of the battles before this it was usual for the anxious staff to wait many hours for information~~ — The counter-gun work against the German guns (themselves countering the tanks) was also very successful today. The following is a report of an action forget of a aeroplane: — counter-gun

(page 231)

The Last 100 Days.

Tanks In Action.

By HENRY WILLIAMSON.

Winner of the Hawthornden Prize for 1928, who is describing on the appropriate tenth anniversaries the chief events of the last phases of the Great War.

August 23, 1918.

This morning at 4.45 hours the ghastly light of the moon waning over the stricken upland fields was flooded with a flickering false-sunrise, and along a thirty-three-mile front—from our junction with the French to the place where the Hindenburg Line from Queant and Bullecourt joined the old Arras-Vimy defence of 1916—the assault behind the barrage opened with a hundred tanks, and men of the 3rd, 4th, 5th, and 6th Corps.

The German machine-gunners defended their posts with extraordinary heroism (they were always brave troops), often squatting behind their guns and firing until the very moment when they were crushed to earth by the tank lurching upon them at four miles an hour. Every third cartridge in the canvas belts feeding their guns held a copper-sheathed steel-cored bullet; the tanks were pitted all over, and in many places penetrated, by these bullets.

* * *

As usual, many of the crews became delirious in the terrific heat inside the tanks; while in some cases the enemy drenched them with phosphorous bombs, filling them with smoke like cotton wool, which choked the breathing and burned throat and eyes.

The work of the contact airplanes was especially successful to-day. The messages and reports they dropped kept the wide straggling action in hand. The counter-work against the German guns (themselves countering the tanks) was also fortunate. The following report of an action fought by a counter-gun airplane came in towards evening:

No. 73 Squadron.

> At 1.15 p.m. batteries were observed unlimbering and coming into action near Béhagnies. Twenty-four bombs were dropped and nearly 2,000 rounds fired at these batteries, causing the greatest confusion. Several limbers were overturned, and horses stampeded, and the personnel scattered in all directions.

All the objectives of the attack have been reached. The 4th Corps, in the centre, has pushed forward to Bihucourt and Loupart Wood (the few acres of charred and naked stumps on the hill blasted by the 1916 bombardments), while the 6th Corps has captured Ervillers and dug in east of the Arras-Bapaume road.

The 5th Corps, helped by the 3rd, has pushed out its right, and established itself on the hills overlooking Albert. Five thousand prisoners and many guns have been taken.

The Last 100 Days.

"So Why Fight On?"

By HENRY WILLIAMSON.

Winner of the Hawthornden prize for 1928.

September 1, 1918.

This morning at 5.30 a.m. the Australian troops of the Sixth Brigade, after a short bombardment, stormed the village and hill of Mont St. Quentin, a mile north of Péronne, and took Anvil Wood.

Another brigade (the Fourteenth), leap-frogged through the Sixth Brigade, and, having mopped up a few machine-gun posts, entered and occupied Péronne. Only a small portion of the north-east suburbs of the town remains in enemy hands.

This is great news, for Péronne is the key that unlocks the river and canal defence for more than twenty miles, being centrally behind both; and also of the railway system that runs east of the River Somme. It means that the line of the Somme has been turned, and a German retirement to the Hindenburg Line is inevitable. Behind this line is open country.

Ludendorff has announced that this "Siegfried Stellung" is impregnable. It consists of a system of deep trenches in the chalky uplands, with thousands of ferro-concrete machine-gun shelters proof against all but direct hits of the heavier shells; and entered by the shafts from dug-outs ten to fifteen yards underground. Belts of rusty barbed wire, seventy yards wide in places, and half-concealed by withering autumn grasses, protect every trench.

* * *

The cellars of cottages and farmhouses in the villages lying within this zone are almost solid with iron and concrete, splayed for criss-cross machine-gun fire. At its strongest part the Hindenburg Line is seven miles deep; its mightiest defence is the Canal du Nord from Havrincourt Wood to Moevres.

During the past month the British Army in France has taken 57,318 German prisoners and 657 guns. In a fortnight the enemy has been driven back over fortified country which took more than six months of 1916-17 to clear.

Many think that it is now full-stop to our advance, and another dreary winter before the Hindenburg Line; but up north Bullecourt and Hendecourt, powerful cores of machine-gun defence, were taken to-day.

Nearer Arras, the Canadians have been lying down in the fields all the afternoon, resting before an attack on the Wotan Switch line, which is to be assaulted at five o'clock to-morrow morning. If the Wotan falls, the war may end in 1919, for we shall be within striking position of the main defences of the Hindenburg Line. While nearly all our soldiers are worn-out, the German troops are dispirited. Every German deserter says the same thing: Germany has lost the war, so why fight on?

6th article

Last Hundred Days

27 August 1918.

Today the Germany Army Group ~~station~~ commanded by Von Boehm, shaken by ceaseless allied attacks,

~~Running~~ ~~the Germans~~ ~~continue~~ their withdraw ~~to a~~ Dom south, on the

continue their withdrawal from ~~their~~ ~~old battlefields of the~~ 1916

~~Somme~~ the old battlefields of the ~~Somme~~ ~~Valley~~ — land

up, under the ceaseless ~~British~~ ~~and~~ & Allied attacks which, two

ground which years ago, was ~~behind heaved up & raked over, again &~~

~~often~~ known as the "Blood Bath of the Somme" — ~~At night~~ The night is

~~eastern sky~~ ~~battlefields are~~ strangely quiet ~~strangely quiet at night~~: only

the ~~occasional~~ ~~crack of a~~ ~~sniper's~~ intermittent pop of a sentry's rifle, and

~~the~~ stuttering bursts of machine gun fire in the wilderness. There

is no regular line of flares soaring up, to drift down slowly,

spreading a pallid greenish wavering light as they fall; there are

no gun flashes below the horizons, no chromatic whining & buzzing of

heavy shells. Jerry is 'pulling out', leaving rearguards among the

~~the~~ long grass & the rusty wire to ~~fire~~ move up and down

and fire ~~often~~ from so many points, to give the impression

that his trenches are fully held.

The ~~rose red~~ ~~ruddy~~ glow eastern sky ~~lit~~ is

~~a glow with~~ direction of Bapaume and Peronne ~~ruddy~~ lit up with a ruddy glow a fiery stain ~~the glow~~ spreads to

~~from~~ the zenith, of burning dumps. Sometimes ~~streaks~~ ~~to~~ ~~hang~~ seeming to hang and

tremble in the sky before sinking down, & rising again. Twenty, thirty,

forty seconds afterwards come the dull rumbles of shells exploding

miles away. The enemy is going far, falling back on the

general line Quéant — ~~east of Bapaume~~ Bois de Havrincourt — Peronne — Ham.

Havrincourt (~~the~~ "mossy face" work of the old R.F.C. in the air, from its resemblance, from the air, to the ace of spades) — east of

Corbie, ...

1 September 1918.

~~This morning~~
Today
Somme has been formidable ~~the~~ Hindenburg
~~This morning~~ the German line on the ~~battered but~~ Line has ~~between~~
now only ~~that~~ battered but ~~....~~ ~~but~~ formidable ~~....~~ the enemy and then actually
defiant behind
turned, and ~~his retreat to that~~ Ludendorff He has announced that
~~the Hindenburg Line is inevitable.~~ it
the 'Siegfried Stellung' is impregnable: it
that ~~this~~
consists of a ~~...~~ system of deep trenches in the chalk, with ferro-
concrete machine gun shelters, proof against all but the heavier ~~....~~
connected
~~....~~ shells, and dug-outs ten yards underground, protected
by innumerable belts of rusty wire in places seventy yards
~~....~~ lying of ~~this~~ within this 'stellung' (position)
cottage and farmhouse
deep. The cellars of the villages
are almost solid with iron & concrete. At its strongest part
~~....~~ mightiest
the Hindenburg Line is seven miles deep: its most ~~....~~ defence is
the Canal du Nord from Havrincourt Wood to Moeuvres;
South of Havrincourt Wood the canal runs south
to Péronne, a distance of about twelve miles, where it joins
river
the Somme. ~~The Australians~~ This morning at dawn ~~the~~ bombardment,
after a short
Australians troops of 6th Brigade,
stormed the village of Mont St. Quentin, a mile north of
Péronne, and both Anvil wood, out of which the
5th Brigade had been driven yesterday. Another Brigade
(the 14th) leap-frogged through the 6th Brigade, &
having mopped up a few machine guns posts, entered &
occupied the ruins of Péronne, only a small portion
of the suburbs on the north-east remaining in the
enemy's hands. [This small but brilliant action may decide the length of the
war.
but unlikely
Péronne is the key to the river and canal defence
for more than twelve miles, being behind lost; and also of the
~~This means that the~~ railway system that runs south behind the Hindenburg
Somme, ~~and~~ ~~the~~ German retreat over the past
Line is inevitable.
month &

For H. Williamson

DURRANT'S PRESS CUTTINGS,

St. Andrew's House, 32 to 34 Holborn Viaduct, and 3 St. Andrew Street, Holborn Circus, E.C.1.

Telephone: CITY 4963.

Daily Express

8 Shoe Lane, E.C.4.

Cutting from issue dated..........26 SEP 1928..........192

MANCHESTER EDITION.

The Last 100 Days.

BREAKING THROUGH . . .

By HENRY WILLIAMSON.

Winner of the Hawthornden Prize for 1928.

September 26, 1918.

All is now ready for the great effort to break through the German armies in the West. Four convergent and practically simultaneous attacks are to be launched almost immediately.

The Americans are to attack west of the Meuse, in the direction of Mézierès; the French, also against Mézierès, in the Argonne; the British are to pierce the Hindenburg Line, between St. Quentin and the Sensee, and advance on Maubeuge; and an Allied force, under the King of the Belgians, is to attack in Flanders in the direction of Ghent.

• • •

All depends on the British attack on the Hindenburg Line in the centre, where a threat to the enemy communications would immediately react on their defences elsewhere. Here, too, the German defence is the most highly organised. A canal, with immensely steep sloping sides, lies through most of the central position.

This morning the French and Americans launched their attack at dawn, after a three-hour bombardment. It was a complete surprise, owing to feint movements of troops and guns during the past week. The 1st Corps, on the left, stormed Vauquois, reached its objectives in the Aire valley, and went forward a little into the great forest of Argonne.

On the right the 3rd Corps crossed the difficult Forges brook, and got to its objectives; but the 5th Corps, in the centre, was held up early in the attack, and so Montfauçon remained in enemy hands, although the 3rd Corps was actually behind the town. Five thousand prisoners were taken.

* * *

The British and Colonial troops further north, waiting to begin their battles, hear the news of this attack with the news from Palestine and Salonika. The Bulgarian Army has "cracked," and is fleeing in what is practically a rout, 10,000 prisoners have been taken, and many guns; while in the Holy Land the Turkish armies are retreating in disorder, their communications cut, and many of their headquarter staffs out of touch with their commands; 45,000 prisoners have been counted, but there are many more straggling about: and much material from the thousands of dumps of ammunition and stores.

Late to-night a very heavy bombardment was opened on the Hindenburg Line, particularly on the wire and machine-gun shelters of the Canal du Nord, the positions of which have been learned chiefly from the wonderful mosaic-photographs taken by the R.A.F. The question worrying all is: Will the tanks be able to cross the canal? If not . . . Meanwhile the sky throbs with light, and the battalions slowly file up to their tape-lines.

DURRANT'S

St. Andrew's House, 32 to 34 Holborn Viaduct, and 3 St. Andrew Street, Holborn Circus, E.C.1.

Telephone: CITY 4963.

Daily Express

8 Shoe Lane, E.C.4.

Cutting from issue dated..........28 SEP 1928..........192

The Last 100 Days.

We Break Through The Line.

By HENRY WILLIAMSON.

Winner of the Hawthornden Prize for 1928, who is describing, exclusively for the "Daily Express," on the appropriate tenth anniversaries, the chief events of the final phases of the great war.

September 29, 1918.

JUST before dawn this morning the 1,600 guns which for two days have been "plastering" the German defences before and along and behind the Scheldt Canal between Holnon and Vendhuile quickened into barrage fire, and the assault on the strongest section of the terrible Hindenburg Line began.

Hindenburg.

We can scarcely hope for success. In some places the canal is dry; in others it is filled with stagnant water six feet deep. Between Le Catelet and Bellicourt it goes under a sloping hill for several miles, between the valleys of the Rivers Scheldt and Somme.

Hidden under cupolas, the Germans wait for our men to advance in the grey mist of this autumn morning.

Their red and green and golden-rain rockets soared up above the mist when the barrage fell like the Niagara Falls upon their positions, and their own artillery behind the canal, in concrete pits, put down the counter-barrage.

No news came in until nearly eleven o'clock. Then we learned that the 9th Corps had met with much success. The 1st Division, advancing south of the bend in the canal at Bellenglise, had established a flank facing south-east from Gricourt to Le Tronquoy tunnel. And, almost incredibly, the 46th Division, which had the hardest task of all, had actually crossed the icy waters of the canal at Bellenglise on their rafts and lifebuoys of kapok hair; and, holding their Lewis guns and rifles above their heads, they had crawled out and rushed the German trench system west of the canal.

Messages began to come in from the contact patrol airplanes. We learn by 3 o'clock in the afternoon that the 46th Division has gone on and has broken through the Hindenburg Line to a depth of three miles, and taken over 4,000 prisoners and seventy guns, at the small cost of 800 casualties!

Then the 32nd Division, leap-frogging through them, has completed the capture of the Beaurevoir reserve line, and by nightfall has taken 800 more prisoners and twenty guns.

* * *

It is marvellous news; but, unfortunately, the other divisions have not been so successful. North of Bellicourt, where the canal went into the side of the hill, the American division met with early disaster. Machine guns were "mowing them down in swathes" below the hill when their tanks came to deal with the "nests."

Late in the afternoon the 5th Division succeeded in reaching the Hindenburg Line at Nauroy, but the Third were held up on the uncut wire.

Nevertheless, the Hindenburg Line is broached, and at last we are in sight of what we have hoped for since that bitter winter of 1914—"open country and the Allemans on the run."

The Last 100 Days.

TOWARDS THE ARMISTICE.

By HENRY WILLIAMSON.

1928 Hawthornden Prize Winner.

October 27, 1918.

THIS evening the bridging preparations for the great Italian drive on the Piave were continued against the Austrian armies.

The British troops of the 10th Army, commanded by Lord Cavan, opened the "push" three days ago by crossing the main channel of the Piave river in small, flat-bottomed boats punted by special Italian troops (pontieri), and driving back or capturing the enemy outposts on the long shoal island of the Grave di Popodopoli.

The general attack should have followed the next day, but the river rose during the night several feet, swirling down at seven miles an hour; and the bridges, by which half a million men and their transport were to cross, could not be thrown across the yellow flood.

Lord Allenby. Lord Cavan.

Last night the engineers at the eleven selected crossing points moved out with their pontoons and bridging gear. The 12th and 10th Armies completed theirs successfully, but on the 8th Army front only two of the seven sets could be established. This morning the bridgeheads on the Austrian bank were made firm, and Cavan's army went forward two miles on a front of four miles, capturing nearly 6,000 prisoners.

* * *

The other armies were unsuccessful. The long, heaving bridges of the 8th and 12th Armies were shot to pieces, and floated away down river, men, animals, and machine-guns with them. The utter failure of the corps on the right wing, which had been detailed to advance in the direction of Vittorio Veneto, has deranged the plans of the whole battle.

The G.O.C. 8th Italian Army, who has the general direction of the attack, decided this afternoon to detach the 18th Corps from his reserves, and to pass it under the command of Cavan's 10th Army. Immediately the movement orders were issued; and towards midnight the fresh troops began to cross over the sound bridges, with the object of pushing north and clearing the front of the troops who are held up.

* * *

On the Palestine front the last fighting of the war took place to-day. During the last five weeks the British armies under Allenby have moved forward 360 miles, destroyed the Turkish armies, taken 80,000 prisoners, 350 guns, and 800 machine-guns.

In France the battle of Tournai-Valenciennes-Courtrai is slowing up, and 10,000 prisoners have been counted. We are now before the great forest of Mormal, for which a "push," which might be the last set-piece" of the year, is being prepared for next week.

Within three weeks (November 14) the Americans are to attack in the direction of the fortress of Metz, in overwhelming numbers; if successful, the war may be over—we believe—by the spring.

The Last 100 Days.

SICK OF THE WAR . . .

By HENRY WILLIAMSON.

October 31, 1918.

AN amazing thing has happened; a thing that the rank and file and the regimental officers of the Allied Armies on the Western Front have given up hoping for during the past two and a half years. Within a week of a "Z" day, the enemy front has been broken, his armies flung into rout, and his Commander-in-Chief has asked for an armistice.

Three days ago the combined Italian and British attack on the Austrian armies across the wide and flooded Piave was in danger of being disorganised owing to the destruction of the pontoon bridges. The British bridges, however, were kept intact, and across these the shock troops of the 18th Italian Corps passed by night and advanced with the British attack.

As the flood water swilled along in its bed more than a mile wide, so the Allied soldiers have swept through the Austrian defence.

The night before last the town of Vittorio Veneto was entered, and 33,000 prisoners were rounded up.

Last night the Austrian troops on Monte Grappa, which had hitherto held firm against many assaults, and had made eight counter-attacks, began to walk away from their positions.

* * *

The announcement from the Austrian command at ten o'clock that "in view of the discussions regarding an armistice between Germany and the United States, our troops fighting on Italian soil have been ordered to evacuate the occupied region," seems hardly adequate, especially as General von Webernau, commanding the Austrian 6th Corps, was already asking for an armistice.

To-day he and his staff, blindfolded, were driven in motor-cars to Villa Giusti, near Padua, and discussions were begun. The Allied War Council at Versailles, where the question of a reply to Germany's demand for an armistice is being discussed, has been notified.

Meanwhile the fighting continues, and the armies of the Dual Monarchy crumble away. The Italian 1st and 6th Armies are attacking in the Trentino; airplanes are bombing and machine-gunning the roads, for miles behind their "lines," which are littered with heavy guns, lorries, motor-cars and ambulances, dead horses, field cookers, and tractors.

So sick of war are the Austrians that in places they are not even bothering to set fire to their dumps. Over a quarter of a million prisoners have been taken already, and thousands of guns.

"The war is over," says the Austrian soldier, slipping out of the heavy equipment he has been cursing for the last four years. He fought while his friends were fighting; but no one can fight an avalanche.

H Williamson

DURRANT'S PRESS CUTTINGS,

St. Andrew's House, 32 to 34 Holborn Viaduct, and 3 St. Andrew Street, Holborn Circus, E.C.1.

TELEPHONE: CITY 4963.

Daily Express

8 Shoe Lane, E.C.4.

Cutting from issue dated 3 NOV 1928 192

The Last 100 Days. *November 4, 1918.*

There Is Talk Of Peace . . .

By HENRY WILLIAMSON.

This morning at dawn the 1st, 3rd and 4th Armies attacked the German positions on a combined front of thirty miles, from the Sambre to the north of Oisy and Valenciennes. It is the supreme effort to break the enemy's power to continue fighting.

Within a few hours our troops had everywhere penetrated the enemy positions. In the south, at Catillon, the Sambre has been crossed at 8 a.m.; in the centre, the great Forest of Mormal, thinned here and there by German foresters during the past four years, has been penetrated; in the north the fortified town of Le Quesnoy, naturally protected by several streams lying parallel to our advance, has been surrounded by the New Zealanders.

* * *

The early morning was clear and starlit; but dense mist came up with the dawn, only thinning under the sun's rays at 8.30 a.m. The enemy barrage was heavy before the forest, with much gas; elsewhere it was inconsiderable. The country south-west of the forest, enclosed with thick orchards and quick-set hedges, made visibility difficult beyond fifty yards—the "fringed hem of the Mormal petticoat," as one airman on contact patrol, bringing news of the success, described it.

French villagers state that the enemy in places withdrew a mile from their positions an hour before zero to escape our torrent of shells; in a number of instances whole companies were found, hiding and unarmed, waiting to surrender. Landrecies, however, was taken only after a stiff fight. A German pigeon loft (complete with birds) was captured in the town

Ten thousand prisoners have been taken, and more than 300 guns. By this victory the German resistance has definitely been broken, and this evening their troops began to fall back on practically the whole battle front.

It is difficult to convey the weariness of our own shattered divisions. Since August 8 there have been ninety-six days of almost continuous battle. Every battalion is a ragged composite of drafts from all and every regiment.

* * *

About 2,000 tanks and armoured cars have been engaged since that sweltering August day when the tide turned; nearly 1,000 have been handed over to salvage. Of these, 313 have been "shot up" so badly that they had to be sent to central workshops, which have repaired and reissued 204. Only fifteen have been damaged beyond repair.

So "full out" have the tanks worked that to-night there is not one available for further fighting. The Tank Corps is "bled white." A philosophical general remarked to me that this limb may indicate the state of the whole body of Mars, since the eastern sky is ruddy with the glare of dumps burning far away, a sign of general retreat which may quickly become rout; for Bulgarians, Turks and Austrians are "out of it"; revolution is raising its head in Germany; and everywhere the talk is of an armistice and Peace.

It may be a question of days! The "boys" may be home for Christmas—leaving behind friends who are beyond the reckoning of days, but whom they will remember, in odd, still moments, all the rest of their lives.

These articles were printed in the *Daily Express* in 1928 and we are grateful for permission to reprint them here: also 'I Believe in the Men Who Died' from the previous item, and the articles in 'And This Was Ypres'.

Further Notes for the *Chronicle*

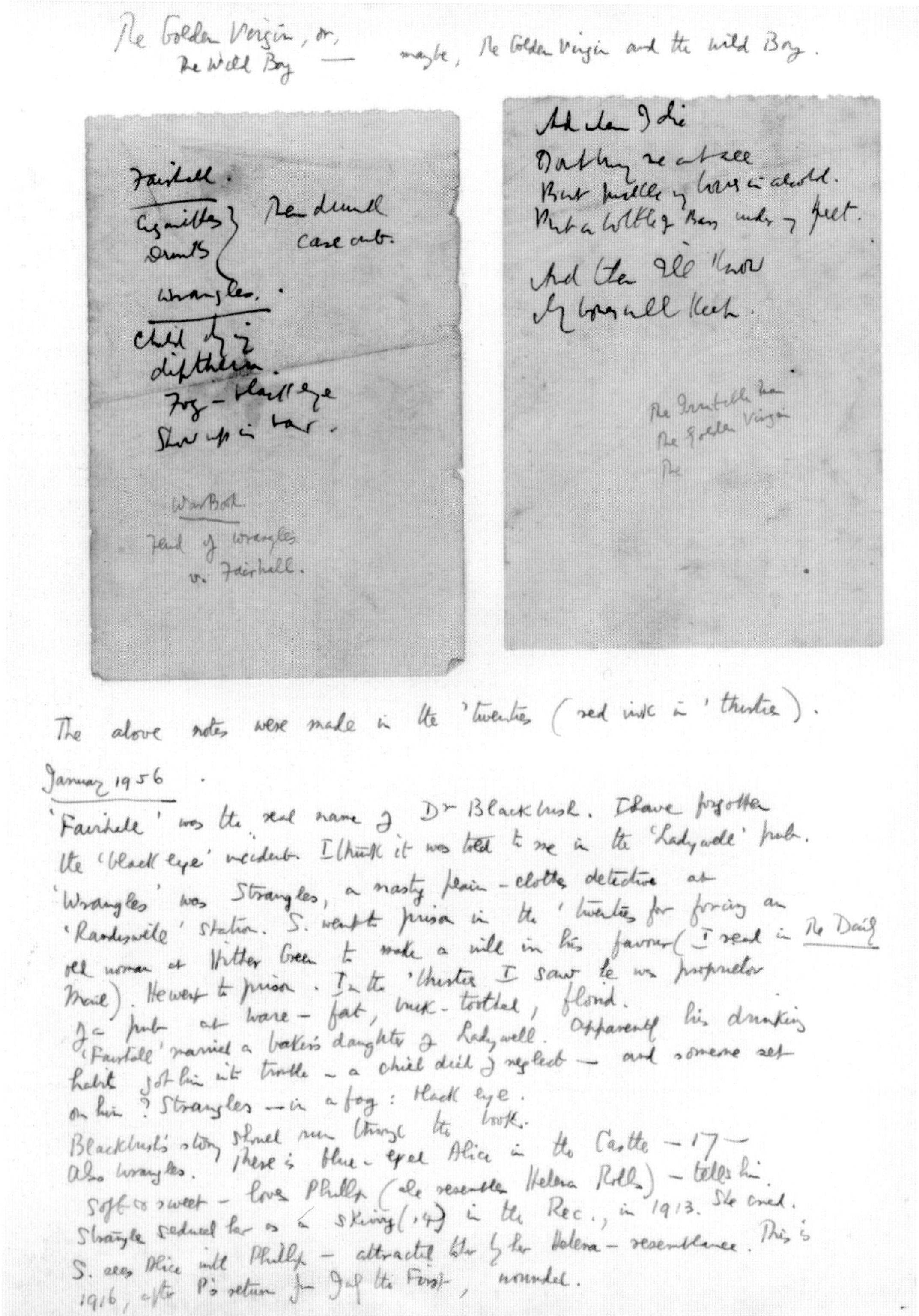

The Golden Virgin, or, The Wild Boy — maybe, The Golden Virgin and the Wild Boy.

Fairhall.
Cigarettes }
Drinks }
Wrangles.
Then dumb case out.
Child dying of diphtheria.
Fog – black eye
Show up in bar.

War Book.
Feud of Wrangles v. Fairhall.

And when I die
Nothing we ask see
But nothing of [illegible] in [illegible].
But a [illegible] under my feet.
And then I'll know
My [illegible] [illegible].

The [illegible]
The Golden Virgin
The

The above notes were made in the 'twenties (red ink in 'thirties).

January 1956.

'Fairhall' was the real name of Dr Blackbush. I have forgotten the 'black eye' incident. I think it was told to me in the 'Ladywell' pub. 'Wrangles' was Strangles, a nasty plain-clothes detective at 'Randiswell' station. S. went to prison in the 'twenties for forcing an old woman at Hither Green to make a will in his favour (I read in The Daily Mail). He went to prison. In the 'thirties I saw he was proprietor of a pub at Ware – fat, buck-toothed, florid.
'Fairhall' married a baker's daughter of Ladywell. Apparently his drinking habit got him into trouble – a child died of neglect – and someone set on him? Strangles – in a fog: black eye.
Blackbush's story should run through the book.
Also Wrangles. There is blue-eyed Alice in the Castle – 17 – soft & sweet – loves Phillip (she resembles Helena Rolls) – tells him. Strangle seduced her as a skivvy (14) in the Rec., in 1913. She cried.
S. sees Alice with Phillip – attracted to her by her Helena-resemblance. This is 1916, after P's return from July the First, wounded.

"You won't forget to write a letter for me old mother, will you sir?" ["I'll do it when I come back," Twinkle.]

461.

(Well, good luck to him!)

part of the battlefield could be overlooked from Maroc, a village in part of which the old front line, immediately and still there; for here the right flank of the attack had rested, on a long, grass-grown spoil heap the best part of a mile in length and forty feet high, extending into the German lines, like two slugs side by side, and known as the Double Crassier.

"Keep-ray you want to be careful in Maroc, for snipers watch it, and there's German still on the Crassier" said Twinkle. "Now don't be late tonight, and [illegible] an old man's heart, will you [illegible]?" [Philip felt that he was playing up, that he did not mean what he said; and then he remembered [illegible]

Twinkle, in the morning was his sober, crafty self, playing, with pink and toothless gums, the part of the harmless old grandad. The [illegible] at least two partners [illegible] that Twinkle had [illegible] in Noeux les Mines, and the other in Mazingarbe, [illegible] horseflesh, this sandwich with lumps of other things. This trade in horseflesh sandwiches was prospering, and he made a bit extra each night with his crown-and-anchor board at the Deri-lune.

[The fact was that he was a deserter since August 1914, and had existed in and around large railway yards, beginning at Villeneuve outside Paris with a sack of bully beef as his capital, and joining himself to various working parties of new troops, he had managed by the hook [illegible] to get along [illegible] Havre, thence to and with fresh troops to Abbeville, [illegible] Rouen, attaching himself as cookhouse fatigue, where the grub was [illegible] in Mazingarbe he had settled down as half a [illegible] to act the rôle of a Mad Jack, or the Doolally Tap.

[Meanwhile he was doing all right [illegible] musters in the district [illegible]

truth was that he had seen the face before. He was Mad Jack, the deserter, a year before, he left hanging about in the railway sidings at Villeneuve, with a sack of bully beef as his "own capital," and the alias of Mad Jack, rations". Now he was

Love and the Loveless

A selection of sketches for the cover

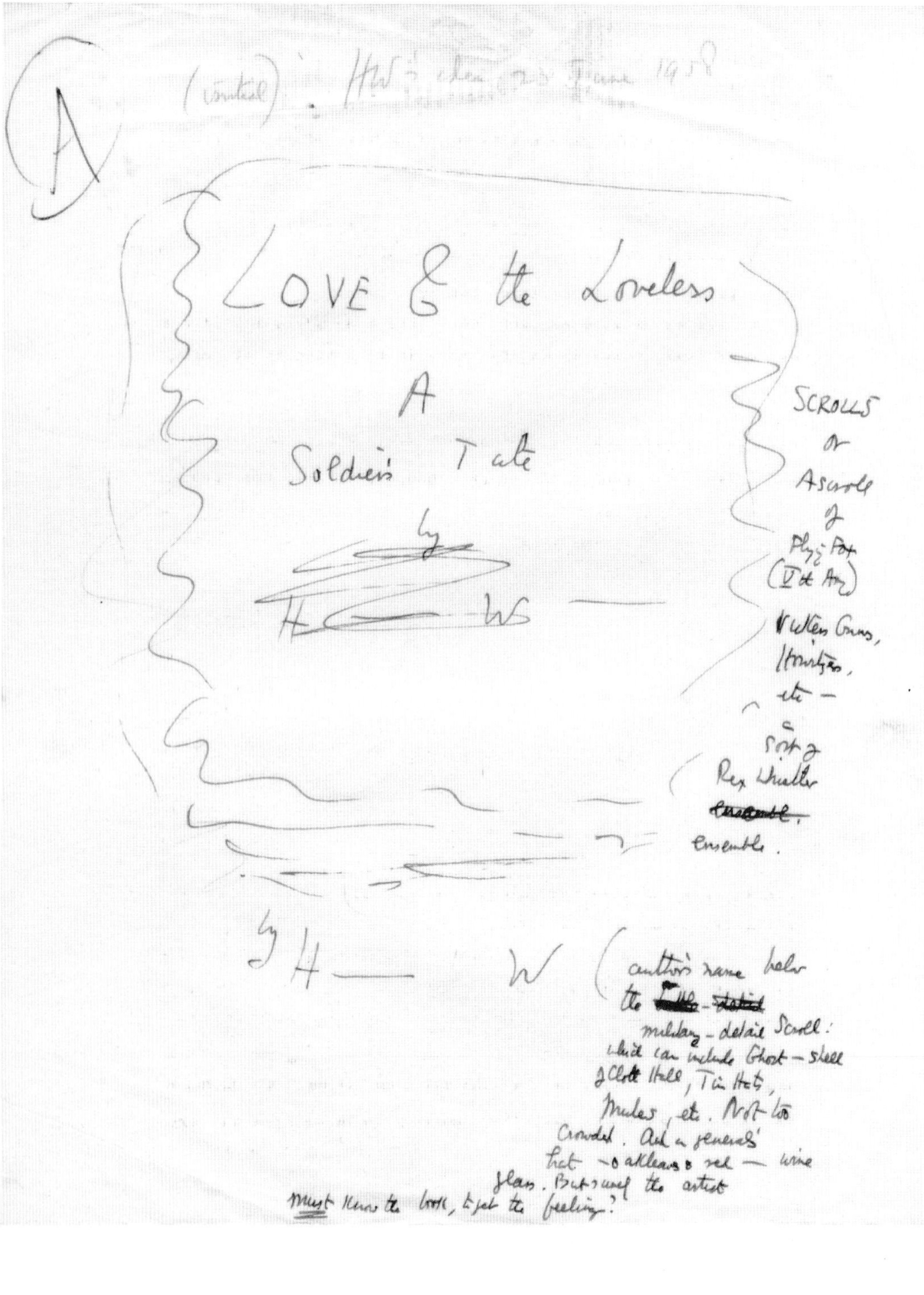

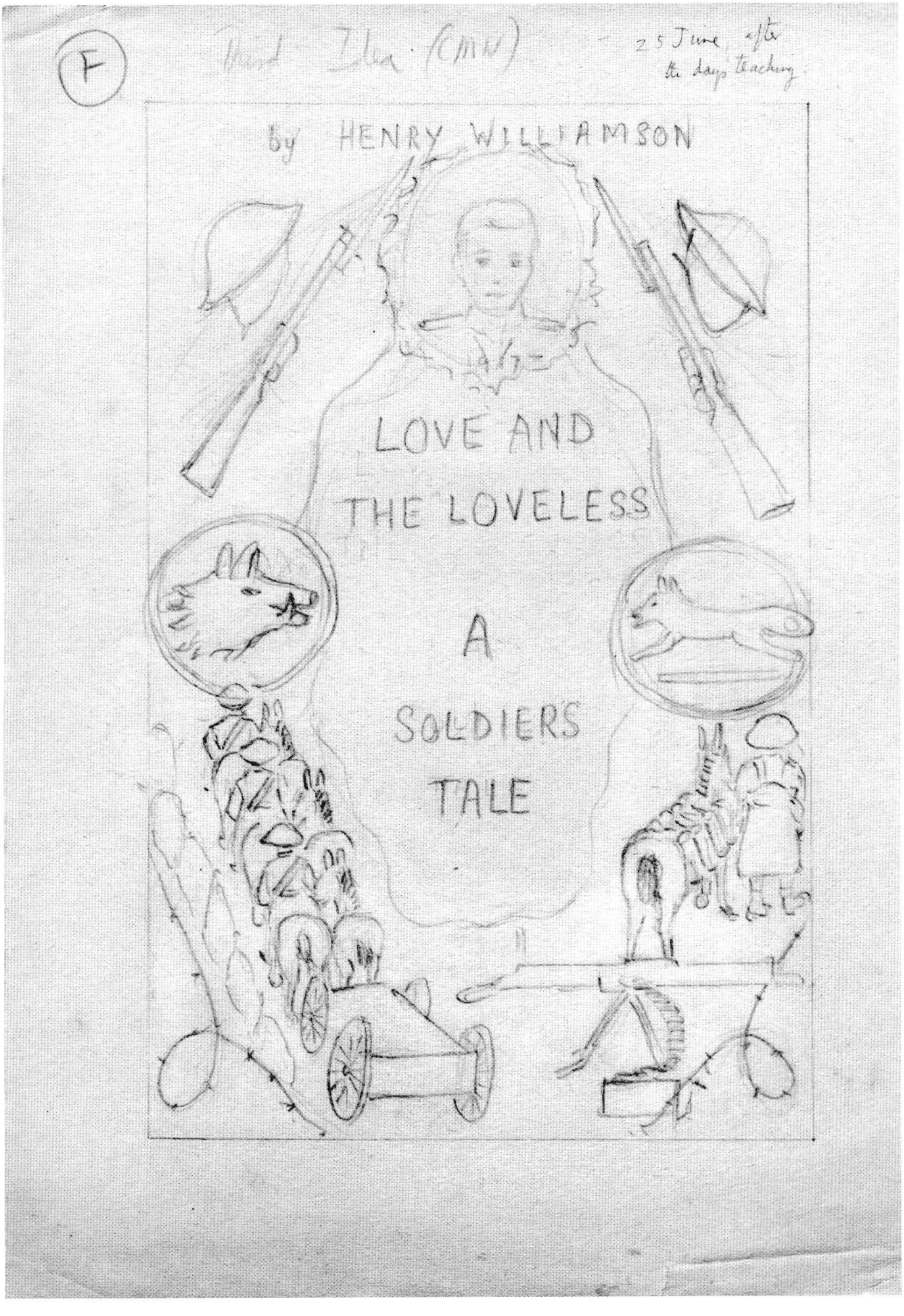
F
Third Idea (CMW)
25 June, after the days teaching.
by HENRY WILLIAMSON
LOVE AND THE LOVELESS
A SOLDIERS TALE

G
4th idea, modified
3-4 July, 9 pm – midnight
HENRY WILLIAMSON
LOVE & THE LOVELESS
A SOLDIER'S TALE

N
HENRY WILLIAMSON
1917
LOVE & THE LOVELESS
A SOLDIER'S TALE

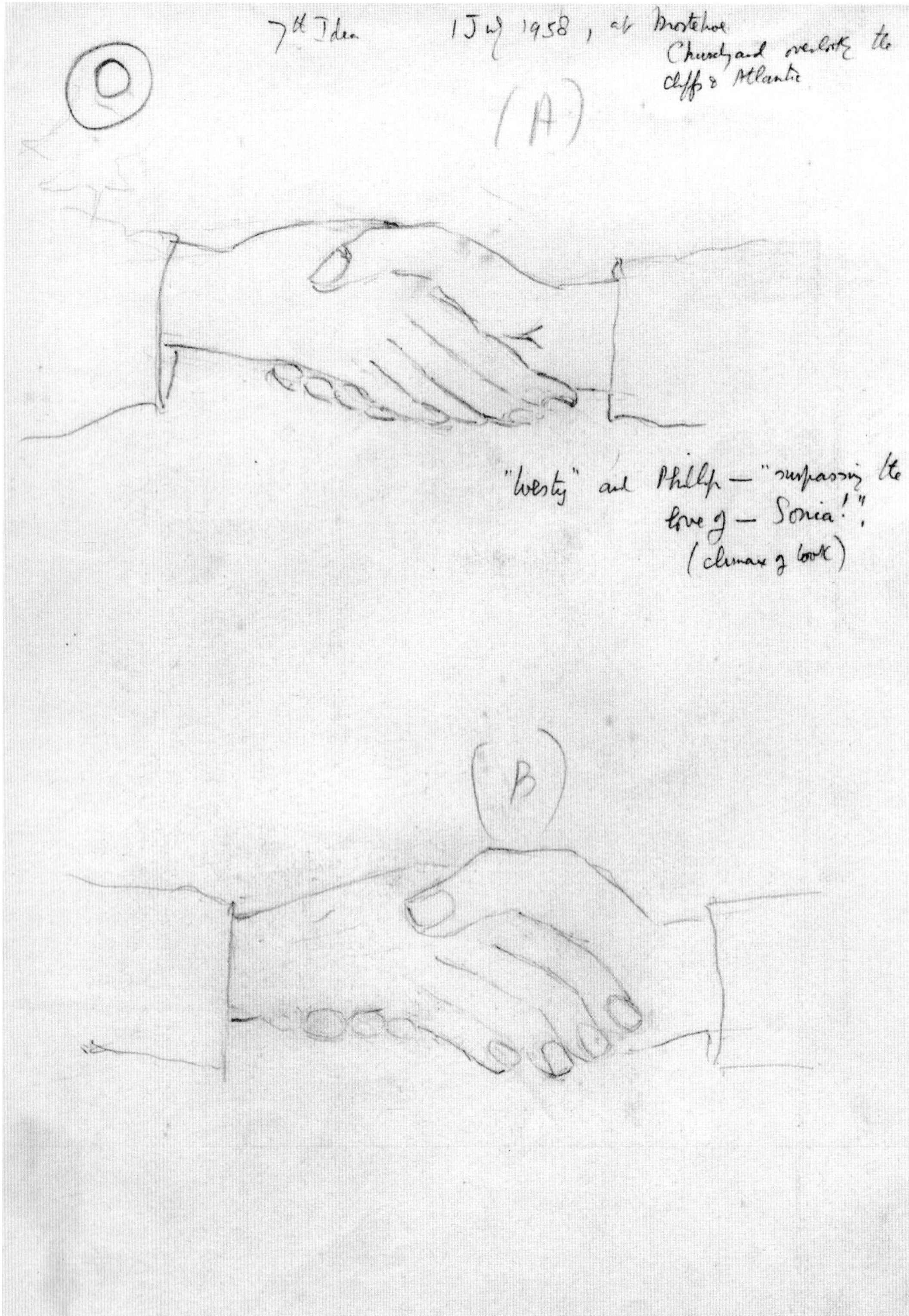
7th Idea 1 July 1958, at Mortehoe
Churchyard overlooking the
cliffs & Atlantic
(A)
"Westy" and Philip — "surpassing the
love of — Sonia!"
(climax of book)
B

Final despairing attempt, 3-4 July, 1am - 3am 4 Jul 1958
HENRY WILLIAMSON
1917
LOVE & THE LOVELESS
a
soldier's tale
The photograph is too small.
This is but a rough sketch, & can be
1917 is unbalanced

113—H. G. LEATES—Contemporary Review - June

REFLECTIONS ON THE DEATH OF A FIELD MARSHAL

by Henry Williamson

I WENT to see *Oh, What a Lovely War!* because I had served as a young volunteer with the infantry in Flanders in the autumn of 1914, and had taken part in the Christmas truce. Later, I served in Artois; on the Somme; and in the Ypres Salient. By the early summer of 1918 I had done with the Western Front and was ~~having a mike~~ on the East Coast until Armistice, when I was posted to a Dispersals Unit at Folkestone. In September, 1919 I returned to the 1st Battalion of my Regiment, then at Cannock Chase, to be demobilised.

The 1914 Christmas Truce in Flanders lasted for five days and nights. Not a shell fell, no bullet cracked overhead. I learned, to my surprise — then being still under-aged — that the Germans in *feld grau* believed the same things that we British believed. While helping to bury their dead lying in Noman's Land, their *Gott mit uns* — in indelible ink on the crosses made of ration-box wood — was the same God on our side. *Für Vaterland und Freiheit* — For God and Freedom! But we British were fighting for freedom, too! Thus my young mind . . .

Our Christmas presents included a brass box from Princess Mary. It held cigarettes and pipe tobacco — the equivalent of the German meerschaum pipe with the Kronprinz on the bowl.

It was amazing to discover we were the same sort of people!

'Englische Prinzessin Mary, her gift to us. Deutscher, Kronprinz Wilhelm! Cousins you see. Your Kaiser — grandson of Queen Victoria, she — very fond of him!'

'Prinzessin! Schön!' replied my opposite number, puffing his Meerschaum pipe. 'Kronprinz Prachtiger Kerl!'

I didn't like to say that Little Willie was a joke with us (from cartoons in the newspapers) for these German words meant 'decent chap'.

Happily we exchanged gifts — a tin of bully beef for a little packet of tobacco. There were many unopened boxes of bully beef chucked away in the wood behind our lines, with boxes of pipe tobacco and cigarettes; the daily ration was said to be 5,000 cigarettes per man, or two pounds of tobacco — all Duty Free Gifts from England, organised by newspapers. As for Fray Bentos bully beef, many trench bottoms were paved by unopened blue tins for hundreds of yards.

The truce lasted until New Year's Eve. The ground was frozen, but no snow had fallen by then. Nor any shells.

The Brighton Rubbish Dump Xmas Day battlefield was all white. Certainly the producer of *Oh, What a Lovely War*! had to do something to hide the old perambulators, tins, pianos, with plastic and cardboard rubbish of the Brighton Corporation . . . but why the black smoke of a shell or two? (Germans, of course, with black smoke). Our 18-pounder shrapnel burst with white smoke; and the lyddite smoke of British 60-pounders was yellowish. There was not one shell falling on Xmas Day in Flanders.

On New Year's Eve a message came over to our lines. We were asked to keep our heads down at midnight, when *automatische pistolen* would fire our way, as the German Regimental (Brigade) staff went round their lines. And at 11 p.m. — Berlin midnight — the machine guns opened up, but the flashes went high.

All through the war on the Western Front few of us had any feeling of hate for the Germans. To hate was the privilege of the Home Front, which harboured revengeful feelings and made the Treaty of Versailles. This was signed the 'the old men' on July 19, 1919, while I was serving with the Dispersals Unit on the Kent coast. I climbed up to Caesar's Camp on the Downs behind Folkestone, and saw the speckles of fire which (one knew) were covering Britain from all along the south coast to Caithness. Beacons glowed on all the hills, the war to end war was over! Sadness — and an indefinable dread — possessed me. Soon I should be back in a lost world of Civvy Street.

The next day I read in one of the papers that, at Versailles Palace, Marshal Foch, late Commander-in-Chief of the Allied Forces on the Western Front, had pointed on the map of Europe at the German port of Danzig on the Baltic, and remarked, 'That is where the next war will begin in twenty years' time!' For much German territory was to be handed over to Poles, Slovaks, Czechs, etc.

Foch was not altogether accurate. September, 1939 was twenty years *and two months* after Versailles. And for some time after the signing, the blockage of Germany continued, while children died of starvation, bread being still half-sawdust. And the French used black colonial troops, who did not behave well. Child harlots were used, or abused. And so Civil war, almost of a private nature began and continued during the 'twenties with scores of thousands of dead.

Oh, What a Lovely War! began well. The preliminaries moved me. I re-entered the life I had known when at school. Here was the feeling we had (from newspapers, deriding everything German) in the years before August, 1914. For the film truly reflects the period of great wealth and splendour when, through our colonies and shipping, we were the Golden Grocers of the world.

But the film says nothing of the lives of two million near-destitute Britons living with no roofs over their heads in Edwardian England's Green and Pleasant Land.

Among the landed families, schooled by inheritance and education *to serve,* were miniature welfare states: schools, churches, village halls, visiting the sick, and pensions for those who had worked all their lives on the estate. But among the aspiring middle-classes of those days ('the Forsytes') the 'lower orders' were considered almost to be a sub-species of that Britain which ruled both the world and its waves.

The film shows us a hint of this as the war darkens into 1917 on the Home Front. We see a Suffragette, Sylvia Pankhurst, pleading for peace from a plinth in Trafalgar Square. I was there, I saw her, I was home on leave from the front. She was jeered by Australian soldiers and others: a brave and tragic figure conveyed in the film by our superb Vanessa Redgrave.

Here let me speak aside. In August, 1914, many babies of Army Reservists called to the colours died of starvation in the slums. Mothers, milkless and near penniless, bought 2d. loaves of white bread which they boiled, to give the warm liquid to their screaming babes.

We heard of this in Flanders from some of the reservists re-called to the Colours — the Regular battalions with whom we Territorials were brigaded. These old sweats, survivors of Mons and Le Cateau, acted as nurses to us all. They were bearded, including the junior and company officers. Quiet voices; a brotherhood of mutual respect and duty. These were the men who stopped the Germans breaking through to Ypres — these pre-war workless who had joined the Army for a shilling a day at a time when the word 'soldier' was a social stigma among the clean and respectable working classes.

> These, in the day when heaven was falling,
> The hour when earth's foundation fled
> Followed their mercenary calling,
> And took their wages, and are dead

wrote A. E. Housman, that classic historian and poet, in his *Epitaph on an Army of Mercenaries,* at the time.

The poem isn't spoken in the film. It was in my head while I watched the sequences on that small screen in Wardour Street, deeming them to be fair enough, though sometimes shallow: the [illegible]e-characterisation of General Sir Douglas Haig, for example: and the apparent eagerness of his lady wife that her husband should succeed the 1914-15 Commander-in-Chief, Field ~~Marshall~~ Marshal Sir John French.

What is the truth? Lady Haig had never desired that her husband should be a senior General. She knew that by such soldiers great burdens must be borne by night and by day. (I have this from the highest authority). Also, surely it was General Sir Douglas Haig's duty to report, after the *experimental* battle of Loos in September, 1915, that Field-Marshal Sir John French had deliberately altered a major item in his Dispatches, viz:- the

[Ed: NB. The marks here are from damage to original sheet.]

time of handing over the reserves — two new Kitchener Divisions — which had arrived by road from St. Omer on Y/Z night, 24/25 September, several hours before the battle was joined; and in an exhausted state.

The march up by night was hot and oppressive. On the narrow roads were many halts. Road control was not possible. Motor and horse'd vehicles, both going and returning, caused traffic blocks. There were deep ditches on both sides of the narrow roads. No lights could be used. Cross-roads caused additional blocks. Battalions had to get into single file. A staff officer wrote afterwards, 'It was like trying to *push* the Lord Mayor's procession through the streets of London without clearing the route and holding up the traffic.'

There were long stoppages at numerous level-crossings, to allow the shunting and running of supply trains . . . for the French were already fighting a tremendous battle, and required priority. And all experience ~~has to be bought with blood and tears, particularly so in war . . . . . . And curses~~.

At Place à Bruay, the 64th Brigade (of the 21st Division, New Army) was held up during 90 minutes; and again at the next level crossing, for 45 minutes of that hot and oppressive night in darkness. There had been, of course, co-ordination, or *liaison*, between the French and British Q staffs; but there was also racial disparagement between French and English.

But worst of all, when the 72nd Brigade (of the 24th Division) commanded by Brigadier-General R. B. Mitford, reached the outskirts of Béthune, the four battalions of the Brigade were halted by a 'Redcap' (Military policeman) because 'the brigade commander had no pass to enter the area'.

And thus and thus the columns marching through a rainy night became ragged, lost, taking wrong turnings which led to retracing steps against the wretched masses of traffic, horse and man become slow and heavy with a first experience of war's reality.

In the small hours of Saturday, September 25, 1915, from 1 a.m. onwards, they arrived, in darkness becoming grey and spectral, at the rear area where soon a few batteries of heavy guns, howitzers, and 18-pounders would rock the world of each man, solitary where he lay in the arable fields besides the roadsides. And abruptly the sky leapt and flickered with light, and the earth beneath each man felt to be the bubbling of a great cauldron.

It was Zero hour — 4 a.m. The battle of Loos had begun. Three hours later, reports came in to First Army headquarters at Hinges that I. and IV. Corps had broken through the first defence system of the enemy. General Haig sent a staff officer by car to G.H.Q., urging the necessity of the XI. Corps being ready to advance in support.

Then another message: I. and IV. Corps had reached the German front-line trenches: and might XI. Corps be pushed on at once?

Two hours had been lost. The 21st and 24th Divisions should have been on the move forward at 6.30 a.m. to follow up the initial assault.

When another hour had been lost, Sir John French yielded to more urgent demands: he moved XI. Corps up the line, but retained the 21st and 24th Divisions 'in general reserve', i.e. under his own orders. This was at 9.30 a.m.

Nearly five hours after Zero Hour the first brigades were on the march up to the battle. Their cookers — ovens and cauldrons on wheels — had been left behind. Some Junior Staff Officer, name unknown, had ordered all transport to be 'massed behind the Divisions'.

I knew that mining country of slag heaps, little villages ('corons') near pit heads and, away in front, whither the little and few roads lay, rising downland; from where everything was overlooked by the Germans, from the fortress of Hill 70.

And in the comparative silence of noon, the position was static. The British attack had been undertaken (by the British War Cabinet's orders) to help the French. The French Tenth Army, away to the north, had failed to take their objective, the Vimy Ridge . . . (The autumn sun was going down behind the battlefield like a septic wound upon a dying world of great loneliness. Weary files of laden men in greatcoats trying to move along the margins of a narrow road congested with down-traffic, pocked by shell-craters, and lined with irregular rows of wounded men recumbent and sitting amidst clustering blow-flies).

Sir John French certainly had a case. To push reserves through a narrow gap in the enemy's defences is to have your men 'pinched off'. Yet the Secretary of State for War — Lord Kitchener — had directed that 'the attack be pushed vigorously'.

And when, eventually, the 21st and 24th Divisions were 'flung into the battle' (as the current phrase ran) on Z-plus-1 Day (a Sunday) the Germans had returned to their trenches.

The British lines of advancing infantry broke under fire, and went back in disorder. The Germans were seen to be standing on their parapets, watching them. Our new troops had been asked to do too much, and too soon — unfed, unwatered, untrained. That is why Marshal French had held them back. But in his Dispatches, later, he had apparently forgotten *when* he did this.

A word for Sir John French. He was elderly. He had borne the mental strain of the Retreat from Mons and Le Cateau, in August, 1914, with almost no *liaison* — communication — with the French Armies. Indeed, many British stragglers, with worn boots and near-blank minds, had dropped out during the retreat, after a week of fighting all day and marching back all night. These stragglers were found wandering about by French patrols and shot out of hand as spies.

For the beginning of any war is chaotic. In the rapid advance of the Germans in August and early September, 1914, two German Army Corps (roughly 200,000 men with artillery and all services) were 'lost' for several days by German Main General Headquarters. This led to cancellation of the order to march on Paris, and to the British 'victory' on the Aisne, followed by the French 'victory' on the Marne, as the Allies followed the retreating Germans.

The British advance continued through Flanders to the North Sea, Sir John French reaching Ypres before the German columns; and we held that town. It was gradually rising country, and wooded in places, east of Ypres; and then *in October* began the battle which went on night and day with massed attacks by the Germans, and that is where we Territorials came in, and marvelled at the calmness of the bearded Regular soldiers, men and officers alike, and never a harsh word in the wood which we held until the battle ended in mid-November and the rains came and we were up to our waists in icy yellow water, and when it froze our boots felt solid, our finger nails pierced by thorns, our greatcoats stiff and heavy as boards; and tears froze on the cheek-bones of many a 17- and 18-year solidier feeling that he was lost for ever and for ever as he tried to sleep upon the hard ground.

The old soldier is a haunted man.

Those nightmare mass-attacks — the sky dilating and roaring with light north and south of the Menin-Ypres road looked a bit different from what we heard on Xmas Day, 1914, a few weeks after the battle had ended in German failure.

'We had one rifle among three *kamaraden*, Herr Englander,' explained a dark-eyed youth with a wispy goatee beard. 'We were students only, and volunteers. Your *automatisch pistolen* were too many for us.'

I learned later that not one Maxim gun remained in operation, after the battle, with the B.E.F. All had been knocked out; including two modern Vickers guns, privately bought before the war by the 14th Battalion of the London Regiment.

What our 'opposite numbers' had mistaken for machine-gun fire into their massed ranks was the 'five-rounds-rapid-fire' of pre-war British and Territorial Army training.

(Are you keeping watch on Wenlock Edge, my Shropshire Lad, for the rest of your 1914 *Epitaph on an Army of Mercenaries*?).

Their shoulders held the sky suspended;
They stood, and earth's foundations stay;
What God abandoned, these defended,
And saved the sum of things for pay.

Those eye-staring, dry-throated attacks on barbed wire, across level No-man's Land, starting early in 1915, in Artois . . . across watery levels the German wire was plain to see; and it was uncut. Our guns had very few high explosive shells. (Later, it came out that Lord Kitchener had decided that shrapnel shells — which explode in the sky and rain down leaden bullets — were the shells required to *cut* barbed wire).

The attacks — to 'keep up the offensive spirit' — were political in origin. They came from the Cabinet to the War House, thence by Chief of the Imperial General Staff to the Commander-in-Chief of the British Expeditionary Force, Sir John French. The attacks, we were told, were 'to relieve pressure on the Russian Front', or, 'to help the French offensive by drawing the enemy reserves North.' So down went the P.B.I. — the 'poor bloody infantry'; and hundreds, thousands of 'officer-material' fell to the mort-blast of the *automatische pistolen* from the Berlin arsenal at Spandau.

Naturally no officer, from second-lieutenant to Field Marshal, wishes to lose his men. Especially on foregone conclusions. So at that battle of Loos in September, 1915, as had been mentioned, the Commander-in-Chief tried to save the exhausted volunteers of New Army men from collapse on that Saturday morning, when we used chlorine gas and some of it drifted back on our chaps. We used 'the expedient', as it was called, because of our lack of heavy guns to destroy the enemy strongholds.

As for the men of the 21st and 24th Divisions, they were obviously not fit to be put into battle.

In any case, the old hero had shot his bolt; and that is what Haig felt it his duty to report. And General Haig was given a Field Marshal's baton.

While the much-praised *Oh, What a Lovely War!* was being made on the Brighton Corporation Rubbish Dump, I had a letter from Mr. Len ~~Leighton,~~ Deighton, then producing the film. We were already acquainted, and Mr. D. wrote to say how much he had learned from my five novels — one for every year of the Great War (as it was called when I was soldiering). I replied that he could make use of any of the facts in the novels for his film. (*How Dear is Life; A Fox under my Cloak; The Golden Virgin; Love and the Loveless;* and *A Test to Destruction* which covers the Home and War Fronts during the five years).

The facts of 'Passchendaele', for example: how, in August, 1917 when, after the brilliant opening of the campaign on July 31 at the Pilckem Ridge, it began to rain; and it rained on during what was to become the wettest summer for 60 years in Flanders. Then the rain ceased awhile; but started again on Y/Z night of the 2nd Battle, and very bad the terrain became thereafter. But Haig had given Marshal Pétain his word that he would keep up the pressure: for, early in August of that year (1917), the Commander-in-Chief of the French Armies had gone to him and told him in confidence that there were 40 French divisions in passive mutiny in and beyond the Champagne area; and should the Boche know of this, he could march to Paris without opposition.

So, having promised help, Haig kept up the attacks in Flanders. There followed seven more battles, all set-pieces like the first which had captured the Pilckem Ridge — a slight rise in the ground near to Ypres, which had overlooked the British positions.

Passchendaele village lay — nearly all of it — in ruins on the eastern horizon, almost seven miles from the Menin Gate at Ypres; and only a little more than half a hundred metres above sea-level. Ypres was below sea-level, but kept dry in normal times by dykes draining water into the canal which was cut east to Nieuport and so through sluices in the sea-wall to the North Sea — great gates which opened as the tide lapsed from the sands, and were closed again by the rising tide.

In that month of August, 1917, so wet, Germany was in sore straits for some raw materials, rubber particularly. She must win quickly; or lose the war. Her gas-masks were of leather, and lasted only a few minutes: steel wheels, with springs only for cushioning, on lorry and motorcar alike.

Britain also was in sore straits: a month's supply of food in the country, for the German submarines were sinking more British ships than could be built. So both armies went for a knock-out.

By November the stump of the church north of the sky-line village of Passchendaele was reached. No longer could the Germans hold their gunnery school on the upper slopes of the ridge whence the artillery cadets had seen below them, during three years, from ground-level slits in their massive concrete *mebus* ('pillboxes' to us) fifty square miles of shell-holes, now lip-to-lip with water. The battlefield was one great morass wherein every single-file wooden infantry track (duck-board) and heavier, wider beech-wood slab 'road' was deep-littered with corpses of animals, broken limbers, and men, added-to nightly to the drone and scream and pulversing roar of bursting shells.

Little or no movement by day: every movement would be spotted: location fixed on gunnery map: ranged within seconds: shrapnel shells sent screaming over from the Gheluvelt ridge on the German left flank, where scores of heavier guns and howitzers enfiladed our wretched, drowned positions.

By November, 1917, all that was ended. We were on the Ridge overlooking, to the east, a new green country — the Plain of Flanders!

How many soldiers know, even today, that 'Passchendaele 1917' caused a German offensive of 30 divisions to be given up — a drive in the direction of Paris? The Germans had missed the opportunity in the spring of 1917 when those French divisions (and a Russian brigade, who had started the 'rot') were in passive mutiny in the Champagne.

Likewise it seems to be not well known what German History has to say about the series of battles officially called Third Ypres, but commonly known in England as 'Passchendaele'. German military historians declare that 'Haig remained Master the Field'. He had destroyed over 80 of their Eingreif Divisionen — each Shock Troop Division averaging, perhaps, 12,000 men.

The German Army, they say, never recovered from the mauling it had received. The German *morale* in the West was low. Ours was hardly better. Mutinies had occurred in several of our Infantry bases, prominently at Etaples. And, as has been said, the French Army was as good as done for. And no wonder, after the appalling slaughter in 1914, only matched by Nivelle's win-or-lose fatal offensive — all eggs in one basket — in Champagne, in the spring of 1917.

We, of the British Fifth Army, heard of that mutiny in May, 1917, when we had advanced out of the Somme morasses to higher green downland — cuckoos calling, larks singing, swallows in the blue sky, butterflies — following the enemy withdrawal to the *Siegfried Stellung* (called, by us, the Hindenburg Line). I was sitting in the Expeditionary Force Canteen, recently erected near Achiet-le-Grand (rebuilt) railway station, with an old acquaintance in the Cambridgeshire Regiment of Newmarket days, when he told me that 'two French Army Corps are marching on Paris'.

The Field Marshal Sir Douglas Haig is said to have been partly inarticulate to visitors calling at G.H.Q. during the war. Politeness, one suspects, led him to listen, rather than to 'hold forth'.

A friend of mine, who served with the 24th Battalion, The London Regiment ~~(Territorials)~~ recently told me the following story. In June, 1916 they were coming out of The Labyrinthe (that place of long and terrible fighting, in 1915, lying east of Lens-Arras road, described in *Le Feu* by Henri Barbusse, the first and finest of the 1914-18 war books).

The sector was now in the British Zone (Third Army) and the 24th Londoners, who had been three weeks in the line, were now relieved, and nearly 'all in', as they went along the road to Arras, some carrying fire-buckets, and other clobber. And, suddenly, there was the Field-Marshal, standing in a G.S. waggon, with members of his staff, besides the road.

The battalion was halted, ordered to close up.

'Be like the Guards', urged the Commander-in-Chief. 'Remember that the Guards came out of action, after the days and nights of the retreat from Mons, with all their ammunition pouches filled. Be like the Guards!'

The story went the rounds that the Guards hadn't fired a shot throughout the retreat from Mons . . . It was a laugh; but the fact was, of course, that the Guards' supply columns were, despite all odds, efficient.

Another story, told to me after the war by Lt. Col. Charlie Foss, V.C., D.S.O., of my Regiment (the 16th Foot). On April 9, 1917, when the Vimy Ridge was taken, in a snowstorm, by the Canadians — a brilliantly successful battle (17,000 prisoners) — Haig motored to Arras. Looking in the direction of the battle he asked 'Where is the Vimy Ridge?'

Charlie Foss, an exquisite painter of wild flowers, seemed to consider this to be an odd enquiry for so eminent a soldier. 'Where is, the Vimy Ridge?' Well, I couldn't see where it was, when I was there in May, 1917. On the map, it lies north of Arras; and so do several other downland risings. And one thinks, which one *is* the Vimy Ridge? And asks a passer-by; to learn that it lies almost due north of the city, is distant about seven kilometers, and on slowly rising ground.

I still can't see the point of Charlie Foss's remark . . . he already knew, of course . . . having been in the very successful British and Canadian assault . . .

I approve, I like the spirit of *Oh, What a Lovely War!*, except for the unknowledgeable scenes where the Madam Tussaud figures of the General Officers prance upon the stage of the Brighton Pier Pavilion. These dummies come only to ventriloquial life; certainly not to truth in the matter of the 60,000 British casualties on July the First, 1916, when the battle of the Somme was joined.

That Saturday was a day of great heat. Pinkish dust from villages, destroyed by bombardment far behind the German lines, hung high in the air. The British 4th Army plan was a slow advance of four lines of infantrymen who were practically carrying parties.

Each line was to walk forwards slowly, at one mile an hour. The objective was the Bapaume Ridge, five miles away to the east.

The idea was to cross a totally destroyed terrain on a twenty mile front which was five miles deep . . . and dig in on the Bapaume Ridge, preparatory to the German counter attack in a few days; to smash the attack with the help of the new-formed Machine Gun Corps, and let the cavalry through into open country. Cavalry, being in effect fast, mobile infantry.

Now German military history records that their Army facing our Fourth Army (which was to fight the battle under General Rawlinson) came near to evacuating the battlefield the night before our assault. Prince Rupprecht of Bavaria, at his Army Group H.G. in Bapaume — a long red brick village built beside the main road — called a conference of all his General Officers, to discuss evacuation by their soldiers before the battle was joined.

Had the British an unknown weapon? How else could the British Fourth Army hope to succeed? For weeks the entire German positions had been under heavy bombardment. From the air, the terrain seemed to be totally destroyed by the new British Ministry of Munitions' batteries of 6-inch howitzers.

But appearances were deceptive. For, unlike the German dugouts in the battle of Loos — two and three metres underground in the chalk — the new German dugouts, linked for miles by tunnels, had 40 wood-cased steps down to a depth of 10 metres, each room wood-cased like the connecting tunnels or corridors. Whereas, the British 6-inch howitzer shell penetrated only about a metre and a half into the top stratum of chalk; and so the dugouts were left intact.

l.c.

move

dig-in

There had been many British raids into the front-line trenches for prisoners to be taken back for identification of units. Could it be that every one of the British reports upon these raids had omitted to state that the new dugouts remained intact under such bombardments?

At this point a German Intelligence officer asked permission to speak. His information was decisive. A message had been intercepted on the German Moritz listening-mechanism. The British Fourth Army Commander had transmitted a message to all troops of his army, to the effect that little opposition could be expected from the German Army on Zero Day — tomorrow.

So, on the morrow, four lines of cumbered British infantry moved slowly forward with the sun in their eyes and keeping line; while in the craters of Noman's Land in places 6-700 yards wide the German machine gunners waited, their Spandau guns pointing east and west, to take the advancing lines in enfilade.

By the afternoon of that day of torrid heat 60,000 men had fallen to the ground. For not one Raid report, of the scores carried out by the British Infantry entering the German front lines during the darkness of June nights, had reported the fact *that there were 40 steps down into the dugouts.*

The Staff wasn't to blame. The information had not been passed on by any of the battalion Intelligence officers. True, Field Marshal Haig had had some doubts. It is recorded that he said to his 4th Army Commander, who was to fight the battle, 'The Infantry Training Manual lays down the principle of "Rush the Position". Have you considered that, Rawly?'

'Yes, Chief, I have,' came the reply. 'There will be little opposition from the Boche front line defences.'

It is a moving last scene in *Oh, What a Lovely War!* — white-shirted and trouser'd youths, wraiths of some of the dead young soldiers wandering back to the South Downs. It might have been below Caesar's Camp, where I had stood alone on Peace Night, July 19, 1919, watching the beacons flaming all along the South Downs. For the dead were with me then, as they are now. And they reappeared in the film, silently; and they were in summery clothes as they sat or lay at the edge of acres upon acres of white wooden crosses; and, as the camera panned, more and more crosses, thousands upon thousands of ghostly crosses, were revealed. And, beside the crosses, but a little apart, stood Haig (played by gentle, compassionate John Mills) a lone, reflective figure.

After the Armistice, and through the following decade, the Field Marshal worked unceasingly to help the unemployed who, having returned from the Western Front in the year of the signing of the Treaty of Versailles, had not found work in the years of 'peace' that followed.

His ideal was that the out-of-work soldiers should be helped by a League of Officers giving their services through the British Legion, founded in July, 1921. By 1928 he was still directing all his energies towards the creation of a new Britain, while the unemployed figures had passed the 2-million mark. Week after week, month after month, year after year the Field Marshal travelled, with little rest, making speech after speech — a voice of the phoenix crying, it might seem, across all the counties where, nearly a decade before, the beacons arose in flame on the hills from Cornwall to Caithness.

Warnings by his colleagues, pleas from his wife that he must rest, were set aside: ~~until one night~~, while he was speaking to a gathering of boys who were helping to make poppies to aid the workless and disabled, he faltered, and turned pale. That night, alone, he died in his sleep, aged 58 years. . . .

And there he was, on guard at the end of the showing of *Oh, What a Lovely War!* in that Wardour Street room, before the general release of the film. There he stood beside the crosses on the graves of those men to whom he was, as one of them who survived can testify, 'Good old Duggie'.

~~But the Field Marshal was not there, on parade, when the film was generally released. I can think of various reasons for the scene being 'cut'. It is better, perhaps for an old soldier, particularly a controversial one, to remain silent!~~

of Britain

lady

Small

d

d

Set aside. "My men did not rest in the war; I do not rest now." Then one evening,

This article first appeared in *Contemporary Review* Vol. 218, No. 1265 (June 1971).

Some thoughts on 'Spectre' West and other elusive characters

Anne Williamson

The real-life prototype of the character Captain Harold West in the war novels of *A Chronicle of Ancient Sunlight*, known as 'Spectre' West or occasionally 'Westy', has intrigued many readers and is one of the main riddles of these books. Dr. J. Wheatley Blench has stated: 'In Williamson's *Chronicle* some of the characters most notably revealed 'in ancient sunlight' are those in the Gaultshire Regiment … . The noblest of these is 'Spectre' West who plays a vital part in Phillip's development. 'Spectre' represents the best of the volunteer officers; he is a brilliant tactician, whose bravery surmounts a bitter hatred and fear of the war.'[1] Paul Reed made a brave stab at identification in his essay 'Henry Williamson and the Kaiserschlacht March 1918'[2] where he investigates the identity of several characters to be found in *A Test to Destruction*, including that of 'Westy':

> *Physically the description of Westy is very similar to Adrian Carton de Wiart VC* [an eye-patch, injured arm and so on] … . *The two remaining contenders are both officers of HW's Regiment – the Bedfordshires. The first is Lieut-Colonel H.S. Poyntz DSO MC of the 2nd Battalion* [i.e. HW's Battalion]. *His career is very similar to Westy's – he was a regular soldier, seeing service at Ypres in 1914 – but his service with the 2nd Battalion was limited, prior to 1918. By 1918, he was the commanding officer of this Battalion – as was Westy – and had indeed seen some limited service as a staff officer. However, some weeks prior to March 21, he leaves the Battalion, is promoted Brigadier-General and commands the Brigade in which the Battalion was serving; Westy does this during the offensive in the* Chronicle.
>
> *The officer that took over from Poyntz when he was promoted to Brigade was one Major Richard Owen Wynne. Wynne is I firmly believe, the real Westy. Born in June 1892 at Moss Vale, New South Wales, Australia, he was educated at Marlboro College and Clare College, Cambridge. He was granted a commission as a regular Army Officer in August 1914, and joined the 2nd Bedfordshires in June 1915. He was a company commander at Loos and fought throughout all the early part of the Somme Battle, winning the DSO for gallantry in July 1916. He was sent on a Senior Officer's Course in January 1917, but it is not clear if he actually served as a Staff Officer, as he rejoined the Battalion in April 1917. For a short period he was an acting Lt-Col commanding the 18th King's Liverpools and in July 1917 he was posted to the staff of 30th Division, as a liaison officer. He then 'disappeared' (possibly to GHQ) but turned up again in the 2nd Bedfordshires in early 1918. He took over from Poyntz as an acting Lt-Col commanding the Battalion and received a bar to his DSO for his part in the March Retreat. Cf. his citation to that of Phillip Maddison in* A Test to Destruction.
>
> (NB. Major Wynne did not die during the war and afterwards returned to Australia.)

Reed's conclusions are reasoned and plausible as an overall picture. That they do not answer the total picture of 'Spectre' West as he is portrayed by Williamson, lies only in the fact that Reed has looked for a too literal explanation and has not allowed for the more surreal side of Williamson's nature and writing.

It was with great excitement that when recently sorting a box of ephemeral material of the 1960s in Henry's archive for filing and storage, I found an envelope containing the following important item. It was a cutting from the *Daily Telegraph*, 12 March, 1966, an obituary of an ex-army officer who had died the previous day in a fire at his home Trentishoe Manor at Trentishoe, near Lynton, North Devon. The obituary with the heading 'Too Scruffy J.P. dies in fire at home' stated that the officer, Brigadier Arthur Cecil Willison, had fought in the 1914-18 and 1939-45 wars and held the DSO and bar, and MC. The obituary further stated that 'among the debris firemen found hundreds of scorched copies of Brig. Willison's book *The Relief of Tobruk*.' Thus this is the famous Brigadier Willison who led his brigade of tanks and infantry in the breakthrough there in the Second World War and later became a prisoner of war in Italy. The heading at the top of the obituary referred to the fact that Brig. Willison had been removed the previous month from the active list of the Bench of Lynton magistrates because his fellow magistrates complained that he was too scruffy. Willison had apparently replied that his wounded fingers prevented him from shaving. Reports in Devon newspapers were almost identical.[3]

On this sheet torn from the *Daily Telegraph* by Henry Williamson he had written at the top: 'Keep my secret. This is the original of 'Spectre'. Why wasn't I with him?' and again under the heading: "Spectre' West'. The photograph accompanying the obituary shows a man elderly (and indeed looking scruffy and unshaven) with a haunting and haunted look, high forehead and tortured eyes. Under this Henry had written "Arthur Williamson – 1/2 brother (illegitimate)' showing even further his psychological affinity with this man.

This then would seem to be the answer to the riddle, the author himself proclaiming it so. But on investigation the situation proved (once again) to be not quite so straightforward. Brian Dolan soon established from records that Brig. Willison (1896-1966) had served in the First World War with 1 Sherwood Foresters, was on the staff, wounded twice and decorated three times (DSO, MC, & Bar) plus two 'mentions' in Despatches. His highest temporary rank was Captain and he finished the war as a substantive Lieutenant. He later joined the Royal Tank Corps and had a most distinguished army career and was in GSO Intelligence with service in India and the Far East.[4] His entry in *The History of the Sherwood Foresters*, p.203-4 gives slightly more detailed information: '2nd Lieut. The Sherwood Foresters 3.7.1915; Temporary Capt. 19.8.1916; Lieut. 5.9.1916; Capt. 1.1.1923 Royal Tanks Corps. Served with the 1st Battalion and on Staff in the Great War 1914-19, wounded twice, British and Victory Medals, 1914-15 Star, DSO, MC & Bar.'

So far, so good: Willison meets all the parameters that would make him the prototype for 'Spectre' West: his obvious daring and brave personality, his facial characteristics as shown as an old man in the *Daily Telegraph* photograph – high-domed forehead and staring eyes – and the superficial outline of his First World War service (if we allow for use of artistic licence in moving his regiment etc) certainly fit the impression of the spirit of 'Spectre' that is gained from the novels. But there is still lacking real proof.

I have been unable to find any correspondence between Williamson and Willison, although as they lived so near to each other then they may well have communicated by telephone and visits. Willison's son, Lt-General Sir David Willison, who very kindly replied to my enquiry, has no knowledge of any friendship between the two men, stating that his father was totally reticent about his service in the First World War. His only knowledge being that his father was at Sandhurst when war broke out, was commissioned into the Sherwood Foresters and reached France in early 1915. He served mostly with the Hampshire Regiment and was thus known as 'the Ant' for the rest of his life.

However, one of the volumes in Williamson's archive is *The Eighth Division in War, 1914-18*[5]. This has markings against several entries concerning the Sherwood Foresters in the appendix that had previously puzzled me but which now had at least a purpose. These consist of a list of Honours and Awards made (but without any detail unfortunately) and under 'Distinguished Service Order' one finds: 'Lieut. (Int.Off.) A.C. Willison, MC 1/Sherwood Frstrs' and a pencilled note added in the margin 'ANT(RTC)' – the meaning of which was of course revealed by his son's information as above. A further entry records the bar to his MC. The very short pencilled notes against several names are not in Henry's handwriting and may well be Willison's as they are personal and denote detailed knowledge of the people concerned (mainly succinct thoughts on whether they did or did not deserve their decorations!).

The only entry concerning Willison in the actual text is on page 270 describing the final offensive at Mons in October 1918 – some time after the fictional 'Spectre' is drowned in the novel – and is not marked in any way: 'At noon patrols from the 2/East Lancashire and 1/Sherwood Foresters entered St. Amand and after some street fighting occupied the town. 'A' Company 1/Sherwood Foresters were the first to enter the town, Lieut. A.C. Willison, MC, 24th Infantry Brigade Intelligence Officer, being the first man in.' (p.270)

References in the *Official History*, 1915, Vol. II, provide some further details of movements and location of the overall involvement of 8 Division. In September 1915 this consisted of 23, 24, and 25 Brigades. The Divisional Commander was Maj.-Gen. H. Hudson, CB, CIE (1 Aug. 1915–9 Dec. 1916). 24 Brigade was commanded by Br.-Gen. R.S. Oxley and was made up by 1/Worcestershire, 1/Sherwood Foresters (Major l. St. H. Morley), 1/5th Black Watch, 2/E. Lancs and 2/Northamptonshire. On p.262 there is an account of the attack by III Corps/8 Division at Bois Grenier south of Armentieres in September 1915. This is described in *The Eighth Division at War*, chapter IV, 'Bois Grenier' (p.45ff.) as the contribution of 8 Division to the Battle of Loos when 1/Sherwood Foresters were detailed to hold the trenches on the right of the attack. The Official History states that 8 Division casualties were 56 officers, 1342 other ranks. (6) In October the *Official History* notes 1/8th Sherwood Foresters as being with 139 Brigade and on 13 and 14 October were part of attack to reach the Hohenzollern driving the enemy back at all points. The 1/8 Sherwood Foresters took over the redoubt. They lost 25 officers and 405 other ranks.[7] They do not appear to have been with 8 Division for the Somme Battle but in late October 1916 were placed at the disposal of Gen. Pollard for support of Zenith Trench.

So one can pick and choose. Some parts match and others do not. However, it is important to remember that it is most noticeable that 'Spectre' West tends to appear with Phillip in the novels (as can now be seen from Williamson's real involvement in the war) in those scenes that are not based on Williamson's own war service. Thus although Williamson is following an authentic thread through the novels, he himself was not present in these scenes, and despite the case that can be made out for Major Wynne and Lieut. Willison as 'Spectre', *Phillip's* role at these points is fictional, which leads one to assume that 'Spectre's role (whomsoever he was based on) is equally fictional.

Apart from any other consideration, like Alice's pack of cards, the whole scenario as laid out above collapses with the entry in Henry's diary on 30 April 1918: 'Heard Westy died.' This cannot be any of the contendents already mentioned for the role of 'Spectre' West, not even (as Paul Reed notes in his 'Kaiserschlacht' article already cited) Captain J. West, MC, of 4 Bedfordshires – for he was killed on 21 August 1918 in an attack north of the Ancre. This diary entry is the only reference in Williamson's contemporaneous papers of 'Westy' (or any variation of the name) although Henry refers to him in letters to Lady Monica Salmond written in the late 1950s (when writing *The Golden Virgin* and subsequent war volumes of the *Chronicle*) particularly 'I love my poor Westy, who was killed in 1918.' (but Henry may be referring to the fictional character here – not a real person). The identity of this diary 'Westy' is to date a mystery. Brian Dolan has searched records thoroughly and can find no counterpart to fit this entry. It should be stated also that Dolan has found no evidence of any drowning at sea which can be fitted into Williamson's story of 'Spectre' West.

It is necessary to step back from the particular and look at Williamson's overall objectives for his war novels to find some solution of the 'Spectre' riddle. In my Preface to *A Patriot's Progress* I have established that Williamson encompasses an overview of the total war scene within the five books. Although based in large part on his own experience and based on authentic records for those episodes outside his own experience, Phillip's role in the novels fulfills that of the 'everyman' soldier; but Williamson obviously needed also an older and wiser character within the 'heroic' mode to portray other aspects of the war. This is the role of 'Spectre' West and, despite these specific references to his death in 1918, he is no doubt based on more than one real life person, possibly a mixture of all those mentioned above plus other elements not yet discovered (like a painter mixing several colours to achieve the shade he wants) to provide Williamson with the mix necessary to achieve the effect of character that he wanted – another instance of masterly use of structure.

Henry's use of the nickname 'Spectre' may well derive from the central image of Henry Barbusse's *Le Feu* (see *A Patriot's Progress* where the influence of Barbusse on Henry Williamson is discussed in detail). In particular the opening chapter of *Le Feu* dances all around the idea of spectre – 'bloodless faces', 'pale-faced clairvoyants', 'watchers on the threshold of another world' – and in fact the whole book is one long synonym for the word. Williamson himself used the word 'wraith' repeatedly in *The Wet Flanders Plain*. Henry was haunted by his experience of war.

A potent clue about Henry's purpose can be found in his use of the Tennyson quote on the title page of *A Test To Destruction*: 'He faced the spectres of the mind And laid them: thus he came at length to find a stronger faith his own; ...' These lines are taken from Tennyson's poem *In Memoriam to A.H.H.*, written after the death of his great friend Arthur Hallam in 1833. But Tennyson's purpose was wider and deeper than just to record the life of a single man, friend and mentor though he may have been. Not completed until 1850 *In Memoriam* grew into a long reflection on thought in the nineteenth century: as Williamson's *Chronicle* is a reflection on the life and thought of the twentieth century. This is an important aspect in establishing Williamson's real purpose in writing the 'war' novels – the 'above and beyond reality' aspect, the encompassing of the total scene, the larger view, which is the central aim of Williamson's work.

Another scenario that proved difficult to match to real life is found in the opening chapters of *The Golden Virgin* concerning Phillip's immediate Company Commander, Captain Jasper D'Arcy Kingsman, of the 25th Middlesex Regiment, stationed at Hornchurch. Kingsman, 'a quiet elderly captain',[8] commandeers Phillip's car, a Swift, for an official visit to Southend to check on and pay the three blind 'nightwatchers' (used for their superior hearing in detecting approaching enemy aircraft) and then invites Phillip to accompany him to 'my place, about a dozen miles away from the salubrious mud-flats' for the night. Williamson did not have a car of any sort at this time – the Swift will have belonged to 'Kingsman' or another officer, with the truth rearranged to make a livelier story-line. The clue given that Kingsman was an amateur racing driver has not proved productive to date.

Kingsman's home turns out to be, as we discover when Phillip looks at the embossed writing paper, 'Tollemere Park'. Kingsman himself is a fairly minor character within the novels. His importance is that this is the place where Phillip meets Father Aloysius and is introduced to the poem *Into Battle* by Julian Grenfell. We learn that the Kingsmans have just lost their son, an RFC pilot shot down during the battle of Loos, and there is a portrait of him on the wall and another of his father, both by famous artists. The other fact we are given is that the family is Roman Catholic.

In attempting to track down Kingsman's real life counterpart and his residence many hares were started, their trails closely tracked by Brian Dolan and myself over many hours of work. Most of the hares died an untimely death as false trails, although almost all had some part to play in the total picture, and cannot be entirely dismissed. This is one of the most complicated and cleverly disguised parts of the whole sequence. Research into the situation at Hornchurch shows that Kingsman did not exist within the real-life Battalion set-up. I had a theory about all of this but needed to find a way of proving it, and with no information that seemed impossible. Then a vital piece of information came into my hands about the source of the actual name, Jasper Kingsman (very kindly and strangely on almost the same day, forwarded by both Peter Cole and John Gillis, both HWS members, to whom I am most grateful) and from there the puzzle gradually unravelled. As Williamson actually tells us in the novel, the Kingsman memorial does indeed come from a slab on the floor in nearby Horndon Church:

'Here lyeth the body of Jasper Kingsman of this parish and
also of the Middle Temple, London, who departed this life the
15th Day of September 1704 in the 86th year of his Age.'

The *Victoria County History of Essex* (Vol. VII) has references for Jasper Kingsman.[9] The gist of these is that Jasper Kingsman bought South Ockenden Hall in 1692. When he died he disinherited his own son and left his estates to his cousin Josiah. These were handed down through a succession of 'Josiahs' and 'Jaspers' until the line died out in 1789 and the estate was sold. *The Golden Virgin* refers to the memorial slab, and tells us that Capt. Kingsman was the last of his line, had been born in India, and no Kingsman had lived there for over a hundred years. So far, so good: the source for the actual name and the general background is revealed (even Kingsman's calling to the Bar) – but not the modern counterpart. Brian Dolan's research has found no Kingsman records in the Army lists.

One line of attack followed was via the trails of 'Tollemere' and 'D'Arcy' (remember the D'Arcy added into Kingsman's full name), as there are just to the west of Chelmsford a group of villages whose overall name includes 'Tolle', easily seen on a map when making a geographical bid for the source of Kingsman's home, one of which is actually called Tolleshunt D'Arcy. Essex Record Office kindly provided a list of names and addresses that fitted the parameters I sent them. Of these, one struck me as a distinct possibility: 'John Henry Salter, JP, of D'Arcy House, Tolleshunt D'Arcy'.

Brian Dolan set to work to research this line of enquiry, which proved most interesting. The easiest route to check was via the clue in the novel of the dead RFC son with the MC. Dolan's search immediately revealed: 2/Lt. (Temp) John Henry Raymond Salter of 54 Squadron RFC, killed in action 13 October 1917. Although two years later than the Battle of Loos death in the novel, one can allow for some poetic licence and disguising factor on Williamson's part, so this was very promising. However, on cross checking Dolan found no connection between this young pilot, who actually came from the north, and the John Henry Salter of D'Arcy House, and as by then I was already following another trail, we decided to rule this out of the equation. Even so, the coincidence is so odd that one wonders if Williamson indeed knew something of these circumstances. The name D'Arcy cropped up in several ancillary lines of enquiry including the name of the wife of Brigadier Willison (Contender for 'Spectre' West) who married a lady called Hyacinth D'Arcy – muddying the waters quite considerably – but those followed through all proved abortive.

Another clue lies in the description of 'Tollemere Park', ancestral home of Kingsman's wife. The house was cream-coloured; two huge pillars rising beside the entrance seen across a lake fringed with reeds; Palladian front to house etc. A second package from John Gillis contained the result of research he had made in 1971, when he made enquiry of Chelmsford Library about the origin of this house. The librarian at that time suggested Hylands House and Park at Widford which fitted Williamson's description exactly. Because the house and grounds had passed into the ownership of the County Council there were details filed about it. This house had been bought by the Hanbury family in 1854. In 1937 a Mrs. Hanbury lived there with her son, who was a pilot in the Second World War and killed in a flying accident early in that war – a sad event, but interestingly suggestive from the viewpoint of this investigation. Mrs. Hanbury died in 1964 and the house and effects were sold at that time including a large number of paintings, of which three were family portraits (Williamson's description mentions a gallery of paintings and portraits) including Major John Hanbury (1664-1734) and Sir John Hanbury Williams (no date). Dolan found no RFC casualties named Hanbury in the First World War, but interestingly Brigadier Richard Nigel Hanbury (1911-71) was Hon. Colonel of 'The Honeymooners' (nickname for the Beds. & Herts. Regt.) in 1967, so Williamson would certainly have known about him and his background, if only through his membership of the Regimental Association. He had certainly seen or visited this house at some point and decided to use it for his purpose in the novel, but the Hanbury family themselves do not appear to overlap with his elaborate scenario.

Another main clue given as to the identity of 'Kingsman' lies in the two portraits actually mentioned by Williamson in his novel; one of the RFC son by Orpen, the other a family group by Sargent. Fred Shepherd (HWS member and Treasurer, whose main interest in life is 'Fine Art') provided me with a detailed answer to this query. The artists are Sir William Orpen, RA (1878-1931) and John Singer Sargent, RA (1856-1925), both of whom were part of the 'official war artists' programme. Looking for a 'father and son' portrait connection Fred found the following: Sargent had exhibited a portrait of the Earl of Wemyss at the Royal Academy in 1909 entitled 'Presentation Portrait' (Henry would have had no problem with adding an imaginary wife and child to this or any picture!) and Orpen had exhibited a portrait of Michael Wemyss at the Royal Academy in 1917. The Sargent portrait was of the 10th Earl, Sir Hugo Francis Wemyss-Charteris, GCV, also with the title Lord Elcho, who had been Hon. Colonel of the 7th Middlesex Regt. (London Scottish) from 1878-1900 – indeed it was Lord Elcho who gave the Regiment its unique Hodden Grey uniform, designed to avoid clan competition via the rival tartans (see the photograph of Roland Barnes) – and was Aide-de-Camp successively to Queen Victoria, King Edward VII and King George V – a 'King's man' indeed! But the Wemyss family are Scottish and have extensive property in Perthshire, where the Wemyss pottery is made and have no connection with Essex. The 11th Earl, Sir Hugo Richard Wemyss-Charteris succeeded his father in 1914. He was in the 1880s a Conservative MP first for Haddingtonshire, Scotland, (1883-85) and then for Ipswich (1886-95) (too tenuous a connection for the purpose here) and was Hon. Colonel 7/Royal Scots in the First World War. Michael Wemyss proved somewhat elusive; he was not actually the Earl's son and no mention of him has been found in peerage details, and he was not a pilot but was in the Royal Horse Guards. So this whole, seemingly promising, evidence turns out to be somewhat tenuous; there would seem to be a connection but there is not enough to be definite proof. However, that there is some further connection will be seen as the tale unfolds.

First, we must note that Williamson particularly mentions in his novel that Kingsman's son was an RFC pilot and Phillip had seen this portrait in the Royal Academy the previous year. Brian Dolan found a book on Orpen[10] which held vital information. This relates that General Trenchard wanted portraits of men of the Royal Flying Corps for propaganda purposes. His ADC, Maurice Baring, was a friend of Sir William Orpen and introduced him to the pilots Trenchard had particularly chosen. One of these was the air-ace Lt. A.P.F. Rhys-Davids of 56 Squadron stationed at Estrees-Blanche. Orpen painted him in September 1917 simply calling it 'Portrait of an Airman'. Rhys-Davids was shot down almost immediately after, in October 1917. (We are told that he always carried a volume of Blake's poems in his pocket in case he was taken prisoner.) Other RFC portraits by Orpen were Lt. R.T.C. Hoidge and Fl.Sgt. W.G. Bennett, also of 56 Squadron and who were also later killed.

We know that Henry Williamson visited the Royal Academy Summer Exhibition on 12 June 1918 in the company of Mrs. Nicholson (see reference in *A Patriot's Progress*) and I think it can safely be said that he 'lifted' the Rhys-Davids portrait (as the most appropriate) for his own use, and added it into his elaborate plot. And to further point the way, this portrait is reproduced in John Rothenstein's book on the war artists which is in Williamson's archive[11] which would have reminded him of its existence. By the time Williamson came to write *The Golden Virgin*, he probably could not remember the name of the sitter, especially as it is not named in sources, thus the actual sitter was probably of no relevance to his story, he was just using the fact of an RFC pilot as background colour.

The other, and to my mind the main, clue lies in the introduction at this point in the novel of Julian Grenfell's poem *Into Battle*. Although there is no proof, I am sure in my own mind that Henry was aware of this poem from its initial printing in *The Times* on 28 May 1915, on the day that Grenfell's death was reported, and that at that time it made a great impression on him and that the slight doubts he expresses about it in the novel come from a more mature point of view – as is now the general view.[12] As stated in *A Patriot's Progress* he certainly had a copy of this poem in his book *Soldier Poets*.

The thundering line of battle stands
And in the air Death moans and sings
But Day shall clasp him with strong hands
And Night shall fold him in soft wings.
(the last stanza from Julian Grenfell *Into Battle*, 1915
The whole poem is quoted in *The Golden Virgin*, p.72)

Another book in Henry's archive is Monica Salmond's *Bright Armour*.[13] Henry used this book as a source for details of nursing and hospitals during the war, but it has a far greater significance than that. Monica Salmond, at the time of the First World War the Honourable Monica Grenfell, was Julian Grenfell's sister (older by five years), both offspring of Lord and Lady Desborough (family name Grenfell). Julian, born in 1888, was the eldest son and heir. Educated at Eton and Balliol, Grenfell was one of a group of young men of particular brilliance, a now legendary pre-war generation. He was an accomplished classicist, and a dedicated sportsman, his forte being athletics. He also had considerable talent for drawing and verse. Bernard Bergonzi states that Julian Grenfell represents the purest embodiment of the Romantic Hotspurian ideal that the Great War produced.[14]

Most of this group of brilliant young men were destined to die in the First World War. These contemporaries included John Manners, Grenadier Guards, killed September 1914; Charles Lister, eldest son of Lord and Lady Lister (Lord Lister having been killed in the Boer War in 1904) who died at Gallipoli in August 1915; Ego Elcho (NB the connection with Earl Wemyss/Elcho[15]); Arthur Asquith, son of the Asquiths (the 'Kingsman' family knew the Asquiths); Aubrey Herbert; Rupert Brooke, who was at Antwerp on 4 October 1914 and who died of virulent blood poisoning six months later after a three day leave at Port Said granted after an aborted landing by the Hood Battalion on Gallipoli, and was buried on the island of Skyros, as Monica Salmond wrote in Gallipoli 1915 (see later paragraph): 'in the island where Theseus was buried, and whence the young Achilles and the young Pyrrhus were called to Troy, Rupert was buried on April 23, 1915, the day of Shakespeare and St. George.'; and also Bernard Freyberg from New Zealand, who became a Colonel in the Hood Battalion of the Naval Division (several of these young men were in the Hood Battalion) and won the DSO with three bars for his 'Gallipoli swim' and a VC on the Somme – wounded nine times in WW1 and twice in WW2. As Monica Salmond shows in *Bright Armour* the titled families of these doomed young men were involved in running hospitals and convalescent homes, and are shown as just getting on with the job in hand, despite the devastation in their lives, playing their part as best they could. Monica was herself a nurse throughout the war, although frequently totally run down and exhausted.

The Hon. Julian Grenfell, DSO, a Captain in the 1st Royal Dragoons, called 'Roughers' by friends and family, was wounded on 15 May 1915 and was taken to No.7 Stationary Hospital at Boulogne with a scalp wound. A few days previously he had visited his sister very briefly at the hospital where she worked at Wimereux. On hearing the news she hurried to see him and reported to their parents that he was doing well and it did not seem too serious. However a relapse proved that it was and Monica herself went to nurse him. Their parents travelled out to France to be with him and also his younger brother Billy (the second son, Gerald William) managed a brief visit. A further relapse on 26 May portended the end. Two months later Billy was also killed leading a charge at Hooge on 30 July 1915.

Apart from Monica Salmond's book, there are several letters from her in Henry Williamson's archive and copies of two small volumes of typed personally produced Memoirs: *This Day: August 4 1914* (thoughts on life as war was declared) and *Gallipoli 1915 – An anthology*, which contains details from letters and diaries of Julian and his closest friends as previously mentioned (and the source of my own information about this group). *Into Battle* is included here, and in *Bright Armour*, in the original version that Henry Williamson used in *The Golden Virgin* 'the rough copy scribbled and hardly altered in Julian's small pocket diary' (see acknowledgement at front of *The Golden Virgin*). There is also a fragment entitled *Sweet Chestnut Avenue*, which describes the family home. One letter states that 'those years form the axis of our lives ... I have been so impressed by your interest in Julian ... I wish Julian could have known your wonderful writing.' Monica Salmond was married to Sir John Maitland Salmond, GCB,

CMB, CVO, DSO, Marshall of the RAF, and their daughter Rosemary married Nicholas Mosley, MC,[16] the son of Lord Ravensdale (Sir Oswald Mosley) by his first marriage, and Henry was godfather to their son Ivor Mosley. (Monica Salmond mentions 'your godson' (her grandson) frequently in the letters.) Nicholas Mosley succeeded to the Baronetcy on the death of his father in 1980.

Henry Williamson's side of the correspondence is of great interest.[17] Although unfortunately it does not reveal any fresh evidence for the problems being addressed here, it does reinforce my thesis that Julian Grenfell and his poem are central to the plot. On Christmas Eve 1956 Henry wrote to ask, rather belatedly, permission to quote *Into Battle*: '... the theme of that poem has been woven into the narrative [of *The Golden Virgin*] ... the search for the wholeness (love) in varying degrees, connected directly with courage, fortitude, and inner harmony in varying degrees ... And drawn also of a young colonel (Lieut. S.R., temp-captain, acting Lt.-Col.) of 26, broken at Querrieux in June 1916 for objecting to the plan of battle. ... 'Spectre' West. ... New characters – the admirable, elderly Capt. Kingsman. His friend the R.C. priest, later padre, who knew Julian Grenfell – whose poem, as I said, is one of the themes. ...'

These letters throw considerable light on Williamson's overall purpose in the *Chronicle* and need fuller examination than is possible here (see Note 17 above). But a statement of particular importance is found in a typescript letter dated 17 October 1957: 'But the completion of the series anyway will take all one's strength, if it remains, ... [and added in ms] I feel, & have felt since 1919, that this work is my destiny: that if it is not done, it may be lost forever. One is but a medium ... the personal being is small & ordinary, a mere vehicle for the spirit of place & time. ...'

There is one other person who cannot be left out of this particular equation although he was not part of it – Henry Williamson's great friend (Sir) John Heygate. Heygate was educated at Eton and Balliol although, born in 1903, of a much later generation. But more importantly his father was assistant master at Eton until 1918, and would have known the pre-war 'Grenfell set', and discussion about them must certainly have occurred. As the Heygate family had property in Southend they may well be part of this sub-plot, and although their role is of no actual importance here, Williamson may have garnered information from them.

But, as can be seen, none of the possible contenders found to date for the role of 'Jasper Kingsman' really fit the picture. It is therefore quite possible (and to my mind almost certain) that the whole 'Kingsman' scenario was set up solely for the purpose of paying tribute to Julian Grenfell and his family – a play within the play. I felt very strongly from the beginning that the Grenfell poem was the central pivot at this point but could not see how this fitted into what is found in the novel. With the help of all the extra information, including Williamson's own words, I think it can be seen that most of the clues point towards the explanation given. As can now be seen Henry Williamson would have known that the 'Wemyss' portraits, although still only tenuously, would have had a connection. The intricacy of this item, a tiny part of the overall scheme, is amazing; no doubt there can be a further refining of the denouement in due course.

Father Aloysius who also features in this scenario – 'such a good man, the priest-in-charge of St. Saviour's in the High Street [Lewisham]' (*The Golden Virgin*, p.69) is an equally hard character to unravel. The actual Parish Priest of St. Saviour's at the time of the First World War was Canon Joseph Bernard Ward (1873-1950) who served there from 1909 to 1950 and was indeed a chaplain in the army.[18] The Williamson family would certainly have known this priest. (We are told that 'Hetty' went to the church secretly to say prayers.) However I have found no clues whatsoever within Henry's considerable archive and again I am sure in my own mind that 'Father Aloysius' as such was not involved in Henry's own personal life. Like 'Spectre' West he appears mainly in those scenes where Williamson himself was not actually present. He is therefore almost certainly a symbolic figure representing that particular aspect of life – standing for the large number of priests who gave succour to the wounded and dying at the Front. There are certainly recognisable aspects of the well-known Father Benedict, whose book *Happy Days in France & Flanders with the 47th and 49th Divisions* is in Williamson's archive, but a reading of that book soon shows that Benedict was not actually Aloysius, although some passages are marked. Particularly the sermon that appears at the end of Benedict's book as Henry's ms note in the front of it shows: '? End of Golden Virgin. Phillip sees the padre & hears a sermon in his church, on the lines of the last page of this book'; and on turning to that last page after the printed words 'no sacrifice can be in vain, and we trust where we cannot trace that "All is well, all shall be well, and He shall make all to be well." EXSPECTO RESURRECTIONEM MORTUORUM ET VITAM VENTURI SAECULI.' Williamson continues in holograph: 'The priest then gave the blessing of the papal cross, and Phillip bowed his head. Phillip can be floating above the watery crater-zones in silence – the silence that now seemed [more deadly –

crossed out] more heart-breaking than the flame and shock of the barrage over Passchendaele.'

A major clue to the identity of Father Aloysius should lie in the quotation ascribed to him on the title page of *The Golden Virgin*: 'Objects of hate are but our own chimaerae. They arise from wounds within us.' If he had a real-life counterpart that quote should be traceable. I have been unable to do so. However, I was very startled to note in a showing of the film *Ghandi* on television in January 1998 that the great Mahatma's last recorded words before his death on 30 January 1948 were very similar in intent – and I rushed to write them down: 'The devils are in our own hearts and that is where we must fight them.' It would be typical of Henry Williamson to take these words of a great saint and translate them to fit his own purpose in portraying the saintliness of Father Aloysius.

To move from the sublime to the ridiculous, there is one minor character who needs to be clarified as he is mentioned several time in Williamson's letters home and who appears in a somewhat unfavourable light in several volumes of the *Chronicle* as Tom Ching. On the inside cover of a book entitled *War is War* by Ex-Private X (Gollancz, 1930) Williamson has written a note explaining that the author is A.M. Burrage (and that he was a fellow member of the Savage Club who was thrown out in the 1930s for alcoholism, dying soon after and further noting that the descriptions found on pages 30 and 35 do indeed describe Burrage) adding: 'Make a character of AMB as the pal of Collins in the LRB – the jokers of Crowborough' and continuing 'The character on p.97 was Thomas Lecount Efford, original of both Effish and Ching.'

Burrage's passage on p.97 reads: 'There was another suburban hero quite as unpleasant as the last mentioned. He was very young which asks for consideration. Thank God I hadn't to face the job at his age. He had been 'combed out' of a Government office, and he must have been the most disgusting bit of work that ever darkened the doorstep. God had provided this human scarecrow [and HW has underlined the following words] with huge staring eyes – which later stood him in good stead – and he used to whimper to me and ask me if I thought it was any use for him to sham madness. I think he had tried every other complaint on the M.O. except leprosy and womb trouble.' Against this HW notes again: 'This fellow is or was, 'Effish' in *Dandelion Days*, doubling as Tom Ching in the Phillip series.'

Thomas Lecount Efford attended Colfe's Grammar School 1907-12. His entry in Leland Duncan's *Colfe's Grammar School and the Great War* states that he joined 28 Battalion, London Regt. (Artists) as a private in December 1916 and 'Served in France at Arras and Passchendaele where he was badly shaken by an exploding shell.' Poor Efford, there must have been so many like him. But at least he has been immortalised!

NOTES

1. Dr. J. Wheatley Blench, 'Bedfordshire in the Writings of Henry Williamson', HWSJ, No.17 (March 1988), pp.29-43.
2. Paul Reed, 'Henry Williamson and the Kaiserschlacht March 1918', HWSJ, No.18 (Sept. 1988), pp.12-14.
3. Copies of reports from Devon newspapers were kindly provided by Jamie Campbell, Reference Librarian at Barnstaple Library, North Devon, who added the information that Willison had been thought 'eccentric' by local people.
4. Information on Brig. Willison taken from *Who was Who 1961-70* and Army Lists 1315a, 1920. Research Brian Dolan.
5. Lt.-Col. J.J. Boraston, CB, OBE, and Capt. Cyril Bax, *The Eighth Division in War, 1914-1918,* The Medici Society, 1926.
6. *Official History*, 1915, Vol. II, p.426.
7. Ibid. pp.386/87/88.
8. *The Golden Virgin,* chapter 3, 'New World', p.54ff.
9. *Victoria County History of Essex,* Vol VII, pp.112, 119. Copies kindly provided by Essex Record Office.
10. Bruce Arnold, *Orpen: Mirror to an Age*, Jonathan Cape, 1981.
11. John Rothenstein, *British Artists and the War,* Peter Davies, 1931. This book includes six paintings by Orpen including 'Portrait of an Airman' and three by Sargent but not the one referred to by Williamson in his novel.
12. See Bernard Bergonzi, *Heroe's Twilight,* new rev. p/b ed. Carcanet, 1996, where the poem is criticised as naïve.
13. Monica Salmond, *Bright Armour,* Faber & Faber, 1935.
14. Bergonzi, op cit. Bergonzi's book is reviewed in HWSJ, No.33 (Sept. 1997), p.76, where his main argument based on the dichotomy of hero (Hotspur) and anti-hero (Falstaff) within war literature is set out.
15. 'Ego Elcho' was Capt. Hugo Francis Charteris (Lord Elcho), born 28 December 1884 and killed in action in April 1916 – who would have inherited the title 12th Earl Wemyss/Lord Elcho. Instead his son Francis David Charteris, KT (1966), born January 1912, succeeded to this title in 1937.
16. In the Second World War, Nicholas Mosley was a Lt. in 2/London Irish Rifles,and fought with the Irish Brigade in Italy, where he was awarded the Military Cross. Information contained in *The London Irish at War,* A History of the Battalions of the London Irish Rifles in World War II (Pub. by London Irish Rifles Old Comrades Association, 1948) and later a Captain in the Rifle Brigade. Research Brian Dolan.

17. I discovered at a very late stage of writing (i.e. the book, *A Patriot's Progress*) that Henry Williamson's letters to Lady Monica Salmond are deposited at Hertfordshire Archives and Local Studies, Document D/ERV C2749 (14 letters from 24.12.'56 - 16.7.'64). I am grateful to the archive staff for making copies available for me and for permission to use these. Copyright of the actual letters is the province of the Henry Williamson Literary Estate. I was relieved and gratified to find that these letters bore out my own thesis about Julian Grenfell – it showed (if nothing else) that I am on Henry's 'wavelength'! As they throw most interesting light on Williamson's purpose within the *Chronicle* fuller examination of these letters will be published in a future volume of the Henry Williamson Society *Journal*.

18. Information from St. Saviour's Parish Centenary 1894-1994, by courtesy of Roger Chandler-Honnor, Deacon at Holy Cross, Catford, and honorary Chaplain to the LIR, who has lived in Catford all his life – who is a friend of Brian Dolan (who by the most extraordinary coincidence was himself married in St. Saviour's Church in November 1950 and was present with his father at a dinNer to celebrate Canon Ward's Golden Jubilee in 1947. A photograph in the Parish History shows them all at the dinner). Canon Ward's nickname in the parish was 'Bunny' and he was described as 'an arresting, magnetic personality in the pulpit' and was known as a bit of a showman. Apparently during the Blitz (WW2) he used to climb to the top of the church tower instead of going to the shelter, to shake his fist at the Luftwaffe. His character and circumstances do not really fit 'Father Aloysius' and I do not think that they actually were one and the same person, merely that Williamson used some of the facts of Canon Ward's situation and transferred them into his complex tale.

I am grateful to Peter Cole, John Gillis, Fred Shepherd and Brian Dolan for their help with information.

A Group of Soldiers

Anne Williamson

The illustration on the cover of this issue, possibly the preparatory drawing for the well-known oil painting 'A Group of Soldiers' by the official war artist C.R.W. Nevinson,[1] is a most powerful evocation of the First World War.

Christopher Richard Wynne Nevinson was born in 1889, the son of H.W. (Henry Woodd) Nevinson, the well-known writer and war correspondent (Africa, Ireland, Russia etc) and his wife, Margaret Wynne Nevinson, almost equally well-known for her suffragette activities in politics and Poor Law Reform. Meiron and Susie Harris refer to them as an 'aggressively Bohemian' family.[2] Nevinson attended the St. John's Wood School of Art in 1906, aged 17, and from 1910-12 was at The Slade, where he made himself a conspicuous 'leading light', clashing with the redoubtable Professor Tonks who advised him to give up art and proceeded to hinder his career wherever possible. (Tonks's treatment was to haunt him throughout his life.) Nevinson then studied further at St. Julien's in Paris, where he shared a studio with Modigliani, met Picasso and became involved with the work of the Cubists.

Nevinson's self-portrait of 1911 and a similar one four years later show a most passionate face with full sensuous lips, large dark eyes – a brooding mediterranean look that apparently went with a 'latin' temperament. (Nevinson was renowned throughout his life for his flamboyant and fiery character.) The only difference between these two paintings is that in the later one the subject has lost the innocent steadfast look of youth and looks out with an ironic gaze.

In 1913 Nevinson became an adherent of the controversial (at that time) Futurist movement and the right-hand-man of the important Italian Futurist, F.T. Marinetti. In April 1914 he assisted Marinetti with a 'performance' on the theme of War. Two months later he was co-signator with Marinetti of a manifesto entitled *Vital English Art: A Futurist Manifesto* published in *The Observer*, 7 June 1914 (and later elsewhere). The Manifesto was an eleven point denunciation of conservative Academics ('passéist filth'), stating the case for a strong, virile English Art with strength, adventure and sport as an essential element in Art. This alienated Nevinson from Wyndham Lewis and the Vorticists, (the movement of which Richard Aldington was a primary instigator) who were working in a very similar mode and were considered *the* foremost radical group pre-war, although he contributed to the Vorticist organ *Blast*.

When war broke out Nevinson, whose poor health made him unfit for the Army, immediately joined the Red Cross and took a course in motor-engineering, and embarking to Dunkirk was attached to the French Army as an ambulance driver and mechanic, gaining the Mons Star. His work was to expose him to horrific scenes of death and suffering. In February 1915 he wrote to the Editor of *The Times*: 'Sir, I have spent the last three months at the Front in France and Belgium amongst wounds, Blood, Stench, Typhoid, agony and death and ... resent your critic writing about "The sowing of wild oats, and managing to enjoy myself despite the war."'

He witnessed the fighting in Flanders, and the entrenchment that led to stalemate. He was making sketches and notes of the war from the very beginning, working them up into full drawings and paintings whenever there was opportunity. The early works show very clearly the influence of the Futuristic style. e.g. *Return to the Trenches*, 1914 and another of the same title in 1916 – rifles pointing upwards and movement suggested by marching feet swept into characteristic futuristic curves.

In 1915 Nevinson was transferred to the Royal Army Medical Corps. During that year, whilst on leave to get married, he painted *La Mitraillaise*, a powerful closeup view of three French soldiers manning a machine gun in a trench, a dead comrade beside them. Sickert called this 'the most authoritative and concentrated utterance on the War in the history of painting', and a columnist on the *Daily Mirror* wrote on 25.10.16 that General Haig thought Nevinson's futuristic war pictures 'the most expressive interpretation of war' he had come across. (In later years Nevinson himself became very anti-war and denied the worth of *La Mitraillaise*, writing to the Tate Gallery in 1925 asking them to withdraw 'the world's worst picture' from exhibition. 'I hope you will burn it'.)

After a serious bout of rheumatism in 1916 Nevinson was discharged from active service and then worked for a while in the RAMC at the 3rd London General Hospital in Wandsworth working with shell-shocked and mentally deranged soldiers. By the spring of 1917 he was applying for permission to return to the Front as an official War Artist and was back in Flanders at the end of June 1917 as an artist attached to the Bureau of Information, writing back to C.F.G. Masterman, one of the officials, that he was 'all about the line North and South, in trenches, balloons, aeroplanes, batteries, dugouts and most of the roads behind the line'. He was very aware of what was due to his official employers and documented the war in a plain, technically accurate and less directly expressive style than hitherto. The reproduction of War paintings in such publications as the war magazine *Land and Water* and the productions of lithographs and drypoint etchings of War subjects for distribution by the Ministry of Information were part of his conditions of service as a War Artist.

One of Nevinson's best known war images is *The Road from Arras to Bapaume* (1917). In earthy shades of ochre and sepia it depicts a stark straight road in an equally stark landscape at dawn, the slight undulation of the road shown by lines across the work, a few tents loom from the haze and there is a little movement of troops, transport and a limber along the road. The sense of disaster and nothingness is intense. Bapaume was the scene of intense fighting and changed hands many times in successive bombardments. Henry Williamson was part of this scene. It could well have been his limber that was travelling the road in that desolate landscape. Other well-known pictures from this period include *Swooping down on a Taube* (1917), *La Patrie* (1916 – bought by Arnold Bennett), *Column of March* (1915) and *A Group of Soldiers* (1917), for which the drawing owned by Henry Williamson may be the original study.

Nevinson and Williamson were friends for several years but I have been unable to establish exactly when the work was exchanged. They were both habituées of the Café Royal but it would seem that they actually met at a party given by Nevinson at 1, Steele's Studio at Haverstock Hill, to which Henry was invited as the guest of his friend John Heygate in 1928. Henry had just won the Hawthornden Prize for Literature and was enjoying a more prominent social life at that time. An account of this party can be found in *The Power of the Dead* (Vol II of *A Chronicle of Ancient Sunlight*), chapter 9, 'Bottle Party' where it is shown that the two men did not like each other on sight – the bridling of two male stags – but obviously this soon changed to friendship. There are not many references to Nevinson within Williamson's archive but Henry referred to him as his friend in an article in 1929, drawing on Nevinson as an excuse for his prank over the village sign at Georgeham[3] and showed his respect for the artist by dedicating *The Wet Flanders Plain* (1929) to Nevinson.

Nevinson stayed with the Williamsons at Shallowford in 1932, signing the visitor's book on the same page as C.F. Tunnicliffe[4] who two days previously had drawn there a sketch of himself and Henry at Lydford Gorge (which they had visited for 'Tunny' to prepare the illustrations for Williamson's book *The Star-Born*). Henry wrote a letter to T.E. Lawrence later that week in which he mentioned that he had just had a 'grand week' with Nevinson, who had been staying with him whilst recovering from pneumonia which had set in after a stomach operation. 'A sad but inspiring semi-wreck of a man. And what a gift for telling stories, always with his gargantuan laughter. Nothing petty, nothing mean, nothing unjust, as I in my niminy, pimminy way am inclined to be. ...'[5] However, three years later, the two men quarrelled irrevocably over Williamson's portrayal of Nevinson as 'Channerson' in his novel *The Gold Falcon*, to which Nevinson took violent offence, although Henry insisted none had been meant.[6]

Henry Williamson also knew Nevinson's father, although probably not very well. They both attended the ceremony to unveil a Memorial sarcen stone to Edward Thomas on the Shoulder of Mutton Hill at Steep near Petersfield in Hampshire on 2 October 1937, for Williamson recorded in his diary that he spoke with 'John Masefield, Walter de la Mare and H.W. Nevinson', and that he gave a 'jolly lunch' for Ann and Bronwen Thomas and their brother Merfyn.

The Imperial War Museum own the actual oil painting of *A Group of Soldiers*, one of several of Nevinson's work in their collection. They were unaware of Williamson's copy until I approached them for information. Jan Bourne, Documentation Manager in the Department of Art at the IWM, informed me that Nevinson was very proud of the painting as he had drawn all the faces from ordinary soldiers he had seen on the Tube returning on leave. Some controversy arose as the official censor did not approve of its subject matter considering it an unworthy representation of the British Army, which incensed Nevinson who retorted that he would not paint 'castrated Lancelots'. John Buchan, at that time Director of the Department of Information, intervened and the painting was passed for censorship.[7]

Without seeing the original of the Williamson version, the Imperial War Museum staff suggest that it is probably an early-state drypoint etching (as this was a usual method for Nevinson to employ) but there are several slight differences between the work owned by Henry Williamson and the finished oil painting, for instance a different number of buttons, slightly different puttee binding, etc. and I personally think it is an original pen and ink drawing – but this must be resolved by experts in due course.

But whatever its technical composition it is a very powerful and haunting work. What is remarkable is that the figure looking out towards us is extraordinarily like Henry Williamson as a soldier in 1917. A copy of the work appeared on the back cover of the first edition of Henry Williamson's book *A Test to Destruction* (Macdonald 1960). A letter in Williamson's archive to the publisher shows that he tried to soak the work off its mounting at that time (presumably for ease of transportation) and thus caused damp damage which can clearly be seen round the edges. Further letters show that Henry was very concerned that the work should not appear with any titling or lettering superimposed, hence its appearance on the back cover only.

There are two books in Williamson's archive connected with Nevinson: *C.R.W. Nevinson* (in Contemporary British Artists Series) ed by Albert Rutherston and introduced by 'O.S.' [Osbert Sitwell] (Ernest Benn, 1925), inscribed 'To Harry Williamson Xmas 1932 from C.R.W. Nevinson & Kathleen' which also has a Christmas card inside of a tipped-in photograph of Nevinson's painting of 'Pan Triumphant' and with printed greetings. Sitwell's introduction is a masterpiece of a mannered 'essaie politesse' – much more concerned about its own literary merit than about Nevinson's life and work, yet if the bones are picked there is some meat. His discussion of the 'war pictures' is certainly worth reading.

The other volume is less personal and covers a range of work: John Rothenstein's *British Artists and the War* (Peter Davies, 1931) inscribed in holograph 'Henry Williamson, Shallowford, 1931'. This reproduces six of Nevinson's more famous works and a similar selection of all the major war artists – including Sir William Orpen *Portrait of an Airman* and paintings by John Sargent – though not the one referred to by Williamson in the *Chronicle* (as already discussed in my 'Spectre' West article).

NOTES

1. Background information on Nevinson is taken mainly from *C.R.W. Nevinson: Retrospective Exhibition of Paintings, Drawings and Prints. Catalogue*. Kettle's Yard Gallery, 1988, which was kindly lent to me by Mrs. Anne Patterson, (Nevinson's niece, her mother and Nevinson's wife were sisters) owner of the Copyright of his paintings.
2. Merion and Susie Harries, *The War Artists*, (IWM & Tate Gallery, Michael Joseph, 1983). Copy of information provided by Jan Bourne, Documentation Manager, Department of Art, IWM. This book gives important information not just on the war artists of both the First and Second World War but also the background of the role of the Ministry of Information War Artists Department.
3. See Anne Williamson, *Henry Williamson: Tarka and the Last Romantic*, Sutton Publishing, 1995, p/b ed. 1997, p.124-5: also HWSJ, No.29.
4. See illustration of this entry in my biography, op cit., p.148.
5. Letter from Henry Williamson to T.E. Lawrence, 12 December 1932, copy in the HWLEA. See reference in my biography, op cit., p.156.
6. Ibid. pp.156-7.
7. Information in *The War Artists*, op cit.

I am grateful to Mrs Anne Patterson for permission to use the drawing reproduced on the cover. I am also grateful to the staff at the Imperial War Museum for their help and courtesy on this matter.

A Critical Approach to
A Chronicle of Ancient Sunlight

J.W. Blench

PART II — THE FIRST WORLD WAR

In the second phase of the narrative of the *Chronicle*, the years of the First World War and their immediate aftermath, Williamson shows the development of Phillip's character between the ages of nineteen and twenty-four; from rather callow naivety to a hard-won early maturity. In the second and third parts of *How Dear is Life* he presents Phillip's military experience up to the end of November 1914, although (as noticed earlier) his initial plan was to include in the novel the first part of *A Fox Under My Cloak* which ends in early 1915 with Phillip expecting a commission in the Gaultshires (drawn from the Bedfordshire Regiment) while on sick leave, visiting his relatives at Beau Brickhill with his mother.

The change from civilian to military life is excellently handled by Williamson. Phillip reports in uniform to Headquarters and Willie, who accompanies him, is able to join the London Rifles. For a week the young men are allowed home at night but then this privilege is withdrawn and Phillip has the strange experience of being billetted in a school. With simple-hearted generosity he volunteers for service overseas 'on lines of communication' after an appeal by the Bishop of London. In contrast Theodora recognizes the coming of the evil hysteria of war leading to lack of truth and she deplores the tragedy of conflict between the cousin nations of Britain and Germany. The sale of the Maddison family land is a cause of bitter regret to her, because had it been retained, Phillip and Willie could have farmed in partnership after graduating at a university. As it is, they have become 'two very young urbanised pawns' in what is 'basically a European Industrialists' War, for markets, Germany being the latest competitor.'[62] After a brief period of training excellently described, Phillip goes to France with his battalion, some members of which are presented well as minor characters. The expectation that duty will be confined to guarding lines of communication is soon proved to be false. The London Highlanders take part in the First Battle of Ypres (as historically the London Scottish did). The battle scenes are marvellously portrayed by Williamson; the reader feels deeply involved in them, even sharing in imagination Phillip's experience of funk. By a happy chance Phillip encounters Horace Cranmer, who as a regular guardsman or 'Bill Brown', is able to return something of Phillip's kindness to him in former years by giving him companionship and practical help. In late November the fighting dies down and Phillip leaves the line, not believing at this time that he could get a commission.

In the first part of *A Fox Under My Cloak*, which as I have pointed out, was originally meant to conclude *How Dear Is Life*, the main episode is the Christmas Truce. Using his actual experience as a base, Williamson constructs upon it a convincing fictional narrative which he integrates successfully into the development of the novel. On Christmas Eve Phillip hears a German soldier singing *Stille Nacht!*[63] which his German nurse Minny had sung to him as a child:

> *The grave and tender voice rose out of the frosty mist; it was all so strange; it was like being in another world, to which he had come through a nightmare; a world finer than the one he had left behind, except for beautiful things like music and springtime on his bicycle in the country.*[64]

On Christmas Day itself he fraternizes with some German troops and imprudently explores behind the German lines on a bicycle. He meets Willie who has understood more of the meaning of the Truce than he has, realizing that each side thinks that God is in support of it as it fights for civilization. Thus there is no real quarrel between the opposing front-line troops. Furthermore, Willie declares that the light which appeared above the German trenches and which Phillip thought was a lantern on a pole was in fact the Morning Star, symbol for Williamson of hope and reconciliation. However the actual destructiveness of the war is brought home to the cousins by personal loss; each has lost a good friend in the fighting; Phillip's friend Cranmer is posted missing and Willie's friend Jack Temperley has been killed.

A change of pace and scene is now introduced. Having fallen ill with enteritis and frostbite, Phillip is sent to hospital and in due course home to England. Granted three weeks leave he arrives at Randiswell (drawn from Ladywell). After his experiences in battle it now seems small, and when he reaches home he withdraws upstairs to weep. This I am sure is very true to life of many young soldiers returning home from the front for the first time. However Phillip revives and goes with Desmond Neville to Freddy's pub (drawn from the 'Castle' in Lewisham High Street). Desmond is only sixteen, but has joined the London Electrical Engineers. The friends are beginning to grow up. Nevertheless Phillip is still unsure of himself sexually. On a visit with his mother to Beau Brickhill while waiting for his commission in the Gaultshires, he finds himself still attracted to his cousin Polly. He gets her to come to his bed, but owing to neurosis is unable to make love.

At the beginning of the second part of the novel (originally planned as the beginning) Phillip's commission comes through, dated 22 March 1915. During an initial training period at Sevenoaks he offers a brooch to Helen Rolls, who refuses it, remaining unattainable. He has still not realized that his suit to her is hopeless. He remains very far from maturity, behaving with cringe-making ineptitude during a training period with a T.A. unit in Suffolk. His brother officers consider him to be a bounder. In a singularly foolish attempt at a joke he sets fire to the Colonel's newspaper as he sits reading in the mess. It is little wonder that in the end he suffers the humiliation of a subalterns' court martial. Fortunately he now does begin to mature, subjecting himself to bitter self-analysis. When he leaves to go back to the front-line, the members of the mess are quite kind to him.

Phillip's life at this time, as is usual in the *Chronicle*, is set in a rich social context. The officers of the Cantuvellaunians (drawn from the Cambridgeshire Regiment) are portrayed with vivid individuality: notably the rich but stupid Baldersby, considered by the middle-aged Brendon to be trying virtually to buy his second pip; the courteous and helpful O'Connor; and among others the agreeable senior officers 'Crasher' and 'Little Willie'.

In the third part of the novel Phillip takes part in the Battle of Loos (September, 1915) as a gas-officer. He has the immense good fortune to meet Captain West (nicknamed 'Spectre') of the Gaultshires and to serve with him. Spectre is to be in many ways a father-figure to Phillip, helping him to conquer his fear, because he himself is afraid and yet is able to steel himself to sustain combat. When Spectre is severely wounded Phillip takes over command and leads his troops to outflank the Lone Tree, a key position, feeling that Cranmer is with him. Furthermore he is able to help his old comrades in the Cantuvellaunians before leaving the line. Excellent comic relief is provided by the scenes involving Phillip's batman 'Twinkle' with his racy cockney speech and droll remarks. However comedy is soon succeeded by tragedy when it turns out that Twinkle is in fact a deserter known as 'Mad Jack' and is shot by firing squad. An element of pathos is added when it is revealed that he is the son of Grannie Nobbs, one of those helped by Theodora in her work in the East End. The story of Twinkle emphasizes the fact that although there may be lighter episodes in the war, its underlying nature is to be destructive of life. The transfer to the Middlesex Regiment for which Phillip had applied before leaving England now comes through and he returns home on leave. Once more he encounters Polly Pickering and being now more self-assured successfully makes love to her on the Hill.

The Golden Virgin is one of the finest and richest novels in the sequence and has been analyzed in depth by David Hoyle.[65] I shall consider it here much more briefly in accordance with the approach I am adopting to the *Chronicle*. At the beginning of the novel (originally intended as the end of *A Fox Under My Cloak*) Phillip is still on leave and is behaving in a foolish and uncontrolled way, coming home drunk at nights and giving his sister Mavis ammunition in her verbal war against him. However a letter arrives from Spectre deservedly praising him for his part in the Battle of Loos and regretting his leaving the Gaultshires.

Returning to duty, Phillip falls under another benign influence; his new Company commander, Captain Kingsman, who invites him to stay at his house, Tollemere Park, near Chelmsford in Essex. Phillip realizes that the Kingsmans are happy people, not broken by the death of their only son serving in the R.F.C. at Loos. Also staying in the house is a Catholic priest, Fr. Aloysius, formerly a curate at St. Saviour's, Wakenham. He helps Phillip with sound counsel and is broad-minded enough to praise the agnostic Thomas Hardy as a naturally religious man and a visionary.

The quality of life in Phillip's mess at Grey Towers is poor, but he is able to escape to London for social amusement. There he meets Frances, Spectre's cousin, who tells him of the high regard in which Spectre holds him. She tells him also that Spectre hates the war and hopes to become a country parson in Gaultshire when it is over.

In the new year of 1916 Phillip goes on a machine-gun course which he passes. On leave once more, he discovers that his father now has an allotment at Joy Farm (its real name). The instincts of the countryman are still strong within him. On a brief visit to Beau Brickhill Polly once more comes to

Phillip's bed, but their relationship remains essentially an immature one. In Freddy's bar however he meets Lily Cornford and a more serious relationship develops. She is a girl with a tragic past, having had an abortion when only fourteen after being seduced by the disagreeably corrupt Detective-Sergeant Keechy. A complication is that Desmond resents what he regards as Phillip's enticing away of his girl-friend and this leads to the first major breach between the friends. Although Phillip does not realize it, in fact Lily is in love with him rather than Desmond. In a significant episode he gives her a delightful trip on his motor-cycle to the countryside which means so much to him — the Fish Ponds on Reynard's Common (drawn from Keston), Knollyswood Park (drawn from Holwood Park) and its lakes. She reacts positively to what she sees, seeming to fit into the countryside, as though she had known it all her life. Impressed by Phillip's knowledgeable conversation, she remarks that he must have studied many books. Disclaiming this he makes the reply:

> *But out in a place like this, thoughts come to one, somehow. I think it is the spirit of the earth, which is hidden under pavements. I had a wonderful time out here when I was a boy, it was so wild and so quiet, the beautiful colours of the leaves and ferns, and if you sat still, you saw the life going on around you, all in beautiful shapes and forms.*[66]

The idyll is short-lived; that night Phillip is recalled to duty as the 'big push' in France is coming. Desmond, who is genuinely in love with Lily, resents bitterly Phillip's attentions to her and parts from him in anger.

Phillip rejoins his old comrades, commanded by Kingsman on the Somme front. By a happy providence Spectre West is senior commander, although as a result of the wounds received at Loos he has lost an eye and a hand. Realizing that Phillip has been unsure of himself, he gives him some kind words of encouragement in private, reassuring him that he *is* good enough for his position and does not need to lie that he has been up at Cambridge. Wise as ever, Spectre sees that the battle-plan is wrong; the German dug-outs are deep in the chalk and will withstand bombardment. A quick rush upon the enemy positions is what is needed, not prolonged bombardment and a slow advance. For voicing these views to General Rawlinson he is relieved of his command and sent back to the Gaultshires.

Before the battle Phillip writes to his mother, describing the march up to the line. He recalls picnics on Reynard's Common and acknowledges his faults, expressing appreciation of the happiness which his parents and family have brought to him. He tells how discussions with Fr. Aloysius have helped him towards a better understanding of true values. This letter shows him to have grown greatly in spirit, but sadly he does not feel equal to sending it.

Although on the eve of the battle the Adjutant says to Phillip "With so much stuff going over it will be a cake-walk", Spectre is proved right and the attack on 1 July 1916 fails, with heavy casualties. Phillip is hit and as he lies in a shell-hole, Fr. Aloysius comes and gives him spiritual comfort. Many of Phillip's brigade are killed, including Kingsman, but he himself survives and is sent home to hospital. Afterwards during leave, he finds that he is now bored by Freddy's bar, as he continues to mature. He gives further evidence of this by purchasing some plants to replace those stolen from his father's allotment. Richard is quite moved by this and significantly Phillip meets his eyes for the first time since he was beaten when three years old for opening his father's butterfly case. Furthermore Phillip finally realizes the hopelessness of his love for Helen Rolls when he learns that she has become engaged to Joe Milton, her former fiancé Phillip's cousin Bertie Cakebread having been killed. Wise aunt Theodora is charmed by Phillip's growing mind when he visits her in Devon during leave. Nevertheless he still has not grown out of making love to Polly, who with Doris, Willie and Percy Pickering have accompanied him to Devon. Later Polly lies that she is expecting Phillip's child; the reader realizes that sadly her feelings for him are much deeper than his for her. After the young people have returned from Devon, the war impinges savagely upon their lives. Percy is killed at the battle of Flers and Lily Cornford and her mother are killed in a Zeppelin raid.

The novel ends on a muted but more hopeful note. Phillip and Desmond make up the quarrel over Lily and Phillip apologizes to Mavis for having been beastly to her. At the funeral of a Zeppelin crew in Essex he cannot accept the local vicar's changing the words of the Burial service from 'our dear departed brothers' to 'these men here departed', saying inwardly: 'Goodbye brothers: Your mortal envelopes lie here on Mother Earth, your spirits drift as gossamer across the sea, to where thoughts of love will help you on your journey to the Sun.'[68] On a brief visit to Tollemere Park he learns that Fr. Aloysius has died of wounds. Fr. Aloysius represents the best of the chaplains in the First World War; kind and wise, he gives his life in the exercise of his priesthood on the battlefield, as for example did the celebrated Fr. Willie Doyle S.J.[69] Chastened by recent events, Phillip resolves to do better in future: 'What Spectre West could do, he could do.'[70]

A new beginning opens for Phillip in *Love and the Loveless*, when he trains to be a Transport Officer with the Machine Gun Corps. Before going on embarkation leave he reads the works of Francis Thompson, recommended to him by Aunt Theodora, and finds that they come home to him. His appreciation of literature is increasing as his mind matures. However, on embarkation leave, he experiences something of the frenetic life of London in wartime when he visits Flossie Flowers's hotel (drawn from the well-known Cavendish Hotel in Jermyn Street, run by Mrs Rosa Lewis).[71]

In France once again, Phillip finds his company is attached to a brigade of the East Pennine Division second-line territorials recently arrived in the B.E.F. He can still be tactless, being rebuked by the Veterinary Officer for saying that the East Pennines are no good. Nevertheless his insight into individuals is deepening. He recognizes that Sergeant Rivett's selfishness in not housing properly two drivers stems from the fact that he 'had not yet broken out of the soft-shelled maternal egg.' Furthermore his power of self-analysis is increasing as he realizes that he himself had been like that 'until he had had the raggings which cracked his self-conceit, or self-conception; and later been lucky to meet men like "Spectre" West and Jasper Kingsman.'[72] In December 1916, walking in the old Noman's-land of Mash Valley where he had been on 1 July, he thinks of the dead who fell there: 'His mother's face came to him, while he thought that the spirit of a million unhappy homes had found its final devastation in this land of the loveless.'[73] He believes that the lack of love in pre-war society has in a sense led to the war. This is a profound reflection which shows that Phillip can now think in an illuminating way on abstract questions.

After another spell in Flanders in Spring 1917 when his popular commanding officer 'All-weather' Jack Hobart is killed, Phillip once more gets leave. He has now had enough of the Machine Gun Corps and requests to be returned to the Gaultshires. Taking a train home, he gets out at St. John's Station (its real name) and walks over the Hill. His continuing growth in maturity of outlook is seen clearly in his realization, as he walks, that an understanding of other people's points of view is of vital importance. The tension he has experienced with his father is in fact similar to the un-understanding of the nations at war. At lunch at home, for which he has thoughtfully brought some smoked salmon and ham, he takes an interest in his father's allotment and listens carefully to his story about the Silvertown explosion at the Brünner-Mond chemical works.

When he returns to the front, Phillip encounters Spectre West again, who continues to be a benign influence upon him. A tragic personality, he confides to Phillip that he does not really want to survive the war. Phillip remembers his frustrated love for his cousin Frances and at the end of the novel, is told by Sasha, a habituée of Flossie Flowers's hotel, that he is a locked-away personality. Nevertheless, when he and Phillip go to the chapel in the hop-loft at Tubby Clayton's Toc H house at Poperinge, Spectre weeps silently. He is in fact a man of profound spiritual feeling and on this occasion he allows this feeling to flow forth in his tears. In contrast to Spectre, who always treats Phillip in a kindly way, Downham, a former colleague at the Moon Office, is very disagreeable to him. He is without battle experience and the reader rejoices that in due course he receives a well deserved come-uppance, when he loses his grip after a bomb attack and is deservedly arrested by his second-in-command Teddy Pinnegar. Deciding that he had a fever he is sent to the M.O. and does not return to his command. Shortly before this he had sent Phillip on a course at the notorious Infantry Base Depot at Etaples. While he is there, mutiny breaks out. This historical fact is vividly described by Williamson, who makes good fictional use of it. Phillip shows resolution and courage by going into the town in a private's uniform so that he can report on the situation there. He is no longer the timid recruit of the First Battle of Ypres! He shows further resolution by defying the stupid Assistant Provost Marshall, Major Brendon, whom he first encountered with the Cantuvellaunians. He seizes his horse to ride to tell Haig about the state of the battlefield and the position of the new German line at Passchendaele, Spectre having been hit once again and thus unable to take back this important information himself. After action at the Battle of Cambrai, in the course of which, in an exciting episode, Phillip loses his way when returning with his Machine Gun Company from the front line, he is sent home to hospital and then to Landguard Fort, Suffolk. He is very grateful to Spectre for arranging that he should be returned to the Gaultshires and not to the Middlesex Regiment. In an attractive scene, Phillip accompanies Spectre on New Year's Eve 1917 on a visit to his parents at their public-house, 'The Grapes', Lime Street in the City of London. There he sees a photograph of Spectre's two younger brothers who, Mrs West tells him, had been killed at Hill 60 when serving in the Post Office Rifles. Spectre had been good to them she says, as indeed the reader reflects, he has been to Phillip. She speaks of his hopes to take Holy Orders after the war, a calling which we feel is in accord with his true nature.

A Test to Destruction is the last of the war novels in the *Chronicle* and in it Phillip faces the severest test he has yet met and triumphs over it. He has now attained a hard-won courage and is recommended for a D.S.O. during the German Spring Offensive of 1918. He is generous and tolerant in his attitude to his amusingly eccentric if difficult comrade, Bill Kidd. Bill is for me and I am sure for many other readers, one of the most delightful characters in the *Chronicle*. Ostensibly something of a *miles glorious*, who refers usually to himself in the third person, and is given to playing the mouth-organ, he is nevertheless brave to the point of rashness. In a memorable episode he infuses some steadiness into very young, inexperienced and nervous troops:

> *... in the grey morning mist as Phillip was going with Naylor along the line, he saw Kidd walking forward to look over the near-level wilderness of the old battlefield extending down to Oostaverne. While he was standing up about two hundred yards in front of the outposts a Fokker flew over low and fired at him. Instead of dodging, Kidd stood still. The biplanes turned and coming down low, opened up again. While bullets kicked up earth all around him, Kidd jerked an arm with two-finger insults at the pilot. As the Fokker flew away, they heard him shouting, "Green Hun, you can't shoot straight! Go back and tell Fatty Ludendorff to put you on a course!" Then lighting a fag he strolled back, to arrive coughing and doubled up, to say after a pause in his rusty voice, "You young Boche-eaters can laugh! Wait till you cop a packet of rotten eggs!" More laughter and cries of "Good old Kiddo!" ... Towards noon the sun, a silver shilling in the early hours, became a gold sovereign. More Maltese-crossed aircraft came over. The young soldiers loosed off with their rifles, and shouted insults in imitation of 'Kiddo'.*[74]

Believing that Bill's bravery merits an M.C., Phillip tells Spectre about it, who advises him to recommend the award, promising to support it.

Another of Phillip's eccentric comrades in this novel, presented also by Williamson with warm good humour is Lt. Col. Moggerhanger ('Moggers') a blunt and coarse ranker-officer whose underlying kindness and decency Phillip comes to appreciate. He saves Phillip from death when a stove gives off carbon-monoxide fumes, and his knowledge from his early years of the habits of farm animals proves very useful when a claim for the death of a pig has to be settled. The pig had escaped from a burning barn but died shortly afterwards. Bill Kidd accepted the farmer's allegation that the pig had died by feeding in the army latrines. However Moggers points out that pigs are 'choosy feeders' and that the pig must have been sick to start with. The result is that a modest *ex gratia* payment is made rather than more substantial compensation.

Temporarily blinded by mustard-gas Phillip is sent home and while in hospital at Husborne Abbey (drawn from Woburn) he encounters the small girl Melissa, who later is to play an important part in his life. No longer does he have the support of Spectre, who has been drowned when the troop ship bringing them home hits a mine in the Channel and sinks. Just as Fr. Aloysius represents the best of the First World War chaplains, so Spectre represents the best of the volunteer officers, hating war and yet doing his duty nobly, bravely and wisely. It is in fact a happy providence that he should die; he is seriously disabled and likely to be more so; he has been unable to win the girl he loves and the reader feels it is unlikely that he would ever be fit enough to be ordained.

As the war draws to a close Phillip feels disorientated and alienated from his family. He feels that he would like to go to the West Country and live in the woods. Nevertheless his mind continues to expand. Attending a Minden Day service (1 August, 1918) he is moved almost to tears while his mind burns 'within ancient sunlight of Somme and Bullecourt, Poperinge, the Bull Ring at Etaples, the white chalk parapets of the Bird Cage, the brown desolation of the Messines Ridge.'[75] He realizes however that such tears are in a sense vain, they cannot bring back the dead physically to life; he remembers the sad comment of Francis Thompson (in his essay on Shelley) on the tears of posterity over the tomb of Keats: 'Never a bone the less dry for all their tears.'[76]

Phillip is invested with his D.S.O. and appropriately lunches afterwards with his family at Simpson's, although his earlier plan had been to meet some military chums. He has done the right thing, but is uneasy about his irresolution in the matter. Calling upon Mrs. Neville later in the day, he encounters Desmond and finds him more friendly. He is engaged now, but Phillip learns in due course that he does not really love his fiancée, his heart having been given to Lily.

After the Armistice Phillip is sent to a Dispersal Unit at Shorncliffe and later to a Rest Camp just behind the Leas at Folkestone. There he has a brief and unsatisfactory affair with Eveline Fairfax, who also plays a large part as Willie's friend in *The Dream of Fair Women* in *The Flax of Dream* sequence. However, his mind continues to grow. While he reads Galsworthy, Hardy and Conrad, it is borne in upon him that he too has the power to write creatively. This is a crucial moment for him. It is enhanced when Willie calls upon him unexpectedly and introduces him to Jefferies's *The Story of My Heart* from which he reads rapturously. The result is that after demobilization in the Autumn of 1919, Phillip begins secretly to write a novel 'with a setting in a far imagined countryside, with imagined characters derived from memories of his boyhood with Percy Pickering and his village friends at Beau Brickhill and others of his own boyhood, including Cranmer.'[77] Writing is to be his true vocation, but it is a long time before he realizes that he must not swerve from it.

At this stage in the narrative the reader is likely to feel that Phillip has passed his 'test to destruction' by emerging from the war with courage and humour. However a more severe test of a different nature now confronts him. The places he loved as a boy are being destroyed; the Seven Fields of Shrofften are strewn with building material for houses. He walks with the sinister Ching up the River Randisbourne towards its source through a tragically polluted and desecrated environment. For Williamson a 'clear water stream' is a symbol of spiritual health and clarity. Conversely, a polluted stream is a symbol of spiritual disease and confusion. The journey, which is conveyed very vividly and with great feeling for the ravaging which nature has suffered there, leads to the disastrous incident in which Ching foolishly and maliciously sets fire to a hut. Phillip quixotically takes the blame for this and is sent to prison for a month. He resigns his D.S.O. and seems to have reached the nadir of his fortunes. However a new life begins for him. He goes to the Parnassus Club in Long Acre, founded to encourage young writers (drawn from the Tomorrow Club) and is helped by his grandfather to become a journalist in Fleet Street. Furthermore, he wants to write a novel of family life to be better than Galsworthy's in that he will try to be more impartial towards his characters, seeking to understand rather than to criticize. Frustratingly, after the death of his grandfather, his uncle Joey Turney burns his grandmother's diaries which he had hoped would help him in his project. Nevertheless, the novel ends on a note of hope. Bidding farewell at the railway station to his cousin Maudie after their grandfather's funeral, Phillip declares:

> *"Keep your heart high, cousin! One day I shall bring back the old faces and the old places we knew, which may seem to have been destroyed, but their spirit is still in the sunlight ..."*

Then comes the final supremely important comment:

> *The train went under the bridge, and he turned back feeling a sense of power with which to face the future, because now he understood what had not always been clear in the past. No man could be destroyed once he had discovered poetry, the spirit of life.*[78]

Phillip has triumphed over his most dangerous test to destruction and is ready to develop his gift as a writer.

NOTES (numbered to follow those in Part I)

62 *How Dear is Life*, chapter 12, p. 165. 63 *A Fox Under My Cloak*, chapter 3, p. 37. 64 Ibid., pp. 37–8.
65 'Why I think Henry Williamson is still worth Reading', *The Henry Williamson Society Journal*, no. 11 (April, 1985), pp. 15–28.
66 *The Golden Virgin*, chapter 12, p. 195. 67 Ibid., chapter 18, p. 273. 68 Ibid., L'envoi, p. 447.
69 See A. O'Rahilly, *Father William Doyle, S.J.: a Spiritual Study* (1920).
70 *The Golden Virgin*, L'envoi, p. 448.
71 See John Homan, 'Flossie Flowers Revealed', *The Henry Williamson Society Journal*, no. 22 (September, 1990), pp. 42–3.
72 *Love and the Loveless* (1958), chapter 6, p. 102. 73 Ibid., p. 104.
74 *A Test to Destruction* (1960), chapter 9, pp. 168–9. 75 Ibid., chapter 16, p. 285.
76 Ibid., see Francis Thompson, 'Shelley', *The Works of Francis Thompson*, vol. iii, p. 15.
77 Ibid., chapter 21, p. 389. 78 Ibid., chapter 23, p. 461.

Acknowledgement: I should like to thank the Henry Williamson Literary Estate for permission to quote from the writings of Henry Williamson in this article.

Reviews

Eleanor Farjeon, EDWARD THOMAS: THE LAST FOUR YEARS, Foreword by P.J. Kavanagh and Introduction by Anne Harvey. First pub. OUP 1958; Rev. p/b ed Sutton Publishing 1997. £12.99. ISBN 0 7509 1337 1

Edward Thomas was born in 1878 and published his first book, a volume of pastoral essays, in 1897. He married Helen Noble and they had three children, a son Mervyn, and two daughters, Bronwen and Myfanwy (Ann). Edward's inherent melancholy temperament and the strain of a huge burden of work, much of which he found uncongenial, led to a breakdown in 1911. The following year while still recuperating Edward met Herbert (Bertie) Farjeon at a cricket week. They became friends and later that autumn Bertie arranged a tea-party which included his sister, Eleanor. Eleanor Farjeon, aged 31, self-confessed 'as immature as a girl of 18' fell deeply in love with Edward Thomas and they began an intimate relationship. Not intimate in the sexual sense for Eleanor has denied any such relationship but perhaps the more intimate because of the lack of such an element. Eleanor was also made welcome by Helen who treated her as one of the family.

A year later Edward met the American poet Robert Frost, who moved to England with his family in 1912 and whose first volume of poetry *A Boy's Will* Edward reviewed with great enthusiasm, as he did the next volume *North of Boston*. It was Robert Frost's friendship and influence that turned Edward Thomas's mind towards his own first attempts at poetry – but it was Eleanor Farjeon's steadfast encouragement that strengthened his resolve. The Frost family returned to America in February 1915 and there was talk of Edward joining them but he felt that would be deserting his country and in July 1915 he enlisted into the Artists Rifles. Eleanor Farjeon notes that once this was a fait-accompli 'the self-torment had gone out of him'.

Edward was not sent out to the fighting in France until the very end of January 1917 when Eleanor deduced from his code of a book title 'Armed Men in Tears' that he was going to Armentieres (about par with Henry's codes!). To begin with he was engaged in duties behind the lines (he had a problem with his feet) but asked to go forward for the Battle of Arras: where he was killed on Easter Monday, 9 April 1917 at the tail end of the battle by the passage of a stray shell fired by the retreating Germans; the pressure created by its passing, sucking out air to form a vacuum, stopped his heart.

In later years Henry Williamson always felt he had actually known Edward Thomas and felt a personal affinity with him, not least because Thomas was killed only a very few miles from where Henry was at Mory on that Easter Sunday and as he recorded in his diary, he could hear the noise of that battle: 'Arras bombardment intensive ... Terrific fire Arras way'.

This new edition (published to mark the eightieth anniversary of Thomas's death) of Eleanor Farjeon's memoire of the four years of their deep friendship, which uses Edward's letters and her own diaries with a linking commentary, is a detailed and poignant portrait that gives us an opportunity to gain an insight into the lives of two extraordinary people.

John Laffin, BRITISH BUTCHERS AND BUNGLERS OF WORLD WAR ONE, First pub. 1988, Reprinted in p/b ed 1997, Sutton Publishing, £9.99. ISBN 0 7509 0179 9

The new edition of this book appeared whilst I was deeply immersed in the preparation of *A Patriot's Progress*, the new book on Henry Williamson's experiences in the First World War. My immediate response was a feeling of extreme anger that anyone can still hold such bigoted views, and the only reason for giving the book review space is to point this out.

It has been fashionable for many years to denigrate Earl Haig – always, as the leader, the main scapegoat. Much of this criticism stems from a facile over-clever hindsight and bigoted view of events. Henry Williamson always championed Earl Haig, particularly in his essay 'Reflections on the death of a Field Marshal' (see this issue), and from my own research into the background of the First World War I have found no reason to disagree with his view. However, my knowledge is really very limited and I suddenly found myself experiencing doubts about the conclusions I had drawn and already written in my Preface to the new book. Then the January 1998 issue of *Standto* (the journal of the Western Front Association) arrived containing a highly critical review of Dr. Laffin's book – and I felt relief. The reviewer, G.D. Sheffield, had appeared in the 1997 BBC *Timewatch* documentary on Douglas Haig, a programme in which Dr. Laffin also took part. That programme had left me with the feeling that the tide had turned for the Field Marshal, that sense was at last prevailing, despite Dr. Laffin's strident protestations. Sheffield states in his review that he is not an uncritical admirer of Haig, but it is obvious that his view is a balanced and considered one.

Sheffield had also reviewed the original 1988 edition, where he (and apparently several other reviewers) found a number of 'sins of omission and commission, particularly [Laffin's] use of evidence, some factual inaccuracies and the dubious nature of some of his interpretations'. Sheffield points out that actual errors of spelling, e.g. of names etc, have still not been corrected despite the several reprintings, and continues gently but firmly to point out that research into primary sources shows that Dr. Laffin's view 'is completely wrong'.

There is certainly a small error concerning Henry

Williamson. In quoting from the 'Apologia' preface of *The Wet Flanders Plain,* Laffin states that Henry Williamson was among the attackers at Orvillers on the first day of the Battle of the Somme. Although such an assumption might have been forgiveable at one time, it would not have been very difficult for Dr. Laffin to check that item in 1997. In 'Apologia pro vita mea' Henry was writing of an experience he had in the bell tower of Georgeham church when the cacophony of the bells transported him into a vision of the battlefield area of the Somme – the fighting in that area covered far more than just the attack known as the Battle of the Somme (even so in a vision he could quite legitimately describe the battle itself). It is rather mean to quibble because in the note accompanying the quote Dr. Laffin states that HW 'an infantry officer throughout the war, wrote some of the best books about it'.

REMEMBRANCES OF HELL: THE GREAT WAR DIARY OF WRITER, BROADCASTER AND NATURALIST – NORMAN ELLISON. ed David Lewis. Airlife Publishing, 1997. £19.95. ISBN 1 85310896 0

Norman Ellison may be known to some of you as 'Nomad' of BBC's Children's Hour from 1945–1963, and he also wrote a number of books, some of which were illustrated by Charles Tunnicliffe. Born in Liverpool in 1893, Ellison developed an early interest in natural history encouraged by an uncle. At the outbreak of war he enlisted into the 1st/6th (Rifle) Battalion, Territorial Force, The King's Liverpool Regiment. The present work is based on a compilation of his diaries and letters from that time which he first put together in the early 1920s and then enhanced with research into the archives of the Liverpool Rifles. He then seems to have had grave doubts about the ethics of publishing his book and proceeded to write to a great number of well-known people asking for their views, but still did not publish although he eventually finalised the work in1958. Ellison held many prestigious posts in the world of natural history and was awarded a Charles Kingsley Memorial Medal by the Chester Society in 1946. He bequeathed all his material – eighteen volumes of memoirs, including his Great War Diary, to the Liverpool Record Office. From whence it has now been retrieved by the editor, David Lewis, who had been encouraged by Ellison when he was a child, appearing in a BBC 'Nomad' Nature Week Quiz in 1946, and whose father had served in the same Liverpool Territorial Battalion – the two men had embarked on the same boat in February 1915 en route to France and the battlefields.

The book is well produced and illustrated with drawings by Ellison and some photos taken by a machine-gunner killed in September 1915, whose mother gave them to Ellison after the war (who later presented them to the Imperial War Museum). A main section is the selection of the letters from 'famous people' – including one by Henry Williamson. Written from Skirr Cottage on 29 June 1929, Henry's short letter is a little obscure and has echoes of the tone found in HW's introduction to Douglas Bell's book: 'The truth lasts ... but genius is very rare. ... Get *Under Fire* in the Everyman edition ...'.

Tony Spagnoly, A WALK ROUND PLUGSTREET, CAMEOS OF THE WESTERN FRONT. SOUTH YPRES SECTION 1914-18. Leo Cooper. ISBN 085052 570 5

David Lewis drew my attention to this book which contains a nice tribute to Henry Williamson – but I have been unable to obtain a review copy from the publishers. However as David sent me a copy of the preface, I will concentrate on that.

In his preface Spagnoly states that his interest in 'Plugstreet' began in 1964 when he read the series of articles in the *Evening Standard* commemorating the war by Henry Williamson, particularly 'A Return to the Wood of Plugstreet', accompanied by a photograph of Rifleman Reuben Barnett, the fifteen-year-old Jewish boy killed on 19 December 1914, who was buried during the Christmas Truce six days later at Rifle House Cemetery. Spagnoly has visited this grave many times since, always laying a pebble on the headstone, a Jewish gesture of remembrance.

'Henry Williamson left me with a deep understanding of his feelings ... [his] words have affected me profoundly and dramatically. ... Many famous personalities and writers who served in the war have pronounced on places having had most impact on them but for me, those articles written by Williamson in 1964 vibrate strongest down the years. "The smell of charcoal ... a woodpigeon calling ... the crunch of hoar frost under my feet"; these words, recalling the smell and sounds of Plugstreet, sum up exactly what the wood means to me today. ... This is the reward of Plugstreet Wood for the sensitive soul. Henry Williamson was right, the memories of the wood on a quiet summer's day stay with you forever. The atmosphere is like a magic balm and the spirit is eternal and abiding.

Thankyou for this tribute to HW, Tony Spagnoly. It is obvious that you are also blessed with a heightened sensitivity – not just because of your words about Henry, but your attitude to the area: 'hopefully this book, this battlefield companion, will not deprive you of the underlying calm and embracing serenity of Plugstreet Wood by outlining some of the more violent and dramatic events that happened in its vicinity during those turbulent years 1914 to 1918.' I am sure your book can only enhance the experience of anyone visiting this hallowed place, and on behalf of HW and the Society, wish it and you every success.